THE CHILD'S STORY BIBLE: NEW TESTAMENT

"We have found the long expected Messiah." John 1

The Child's Story Bible:
New Testament

Catherine F. Vos

New edition
illustrated in full colour
by Betty Beeby

THE BANNER OF TRUTH TRUST

THE BANNER OF TRUTH TRUST
3 Murrayfield Road, Edinburgh EH12 6EL
PO Box 621, Carlisle, Pennsylvania 17013, USA

★

THE CHILD'S STORY BIBLE
by CATHERINE F. VOS

*Entire contents, including illustrations,
Copyright 1935, 1949, 1958, and 1969 by*
WM. B. EERDMANS PUBLISHING COMPANY
Grand Rapids, Michigan, U.S.A.

*Vol. 1, November, 1934
Vol. 2, October, 1935
Vol. 3, October, 1936
One-volume edition, April, 1940
Second edition, August, 1949
Third edition, May, 1958
Fourth edition, October, 1969*

*This English edition is published by special arrangement with
Wm. B. Eerdmans Publishing Company
Grand Rapids, Michigan, U.S.A.
1969*

*New Testament only
Reprinted 1976
Reprinted 1980
Reprinted 1986*

ISBN 0 85151 237 2

★

Printed in Great Britain
Photo-litho reprint by Hazell Watson & Viney Limited
from earlier impression

Dedication

To My Dear Mother in Heaven,
Who Told Me These Stories
When I Was a Little Child,
In Much the Same Way
In Which I Have Written Them
In This Book.

Foreword

Retelling Bible stories is both a painstaking and a rewarding task. By the use of simple and dignified language the author, Mrs. Catherine F. Vos, has in her book preserved the beauty of the biblical narratives and at the same time skillfully brought out the meaning of the scriptural account. Her picturesque, imaginative, and poetic style is in harmony with the dignity of the message.

For such reasons the *Child's Story Bible* is one of the most widely known and used Bible story books. The National Union of Christian Schools is happy to have had a hand in the preparation of this book, which was originally intended for use in the Christian schools. Teachers use it for Bible instruction in primary and intermediate grades.

Parents find that the material is adapted also for home use: for reading to the children and also for placing in their hands for personal reading. Although it is intended primarily for children from seven to twelve years of age, it is eminently suitable for reading to those of a much younger age and it is valued by adults as a Bible history.

The publishers spared no expense to make this volume beautiful and to make it appealing to the child. Large, readable type and full-color art work, help to make it an attractive book. A new element in this edition is the reproduction of twenty-four oil paintings of principal Bible characters.

Telling the story of salvation to those who come after us is a glorious task. Christian faith has its roots in historical events. We trust that the *Child's Story Bible* may be a guide to the authoritative narration of these events, the Book of books, and to Him who said, "I am the way, the truth, and the life."

JOHN A. VANDER ARK, *Director*
National Union of Christian Schools

CONTENTS

CONTENTS

CONTENTS

CHAPTER 1

The Priest Who Could Not Talk

LUKE 1

If you will open your Bible, in the middle you will probably find several blank pages, with no printing at all upon them. At the end of the first part you will find these words —

THE END OF THE OLD TESTAMENT

Now if you turn to the beginning of the second part, you will see that it is called:

THE NEW TESTAMENT

Between the two writings there was a long time when nothing was added to the Bible. After the Old Testament was finished, four hundred years passed before the New Testament was begun.

What happened to the Jewish people in those four hundred years? The Bible does not tell us, but we can find out by reading some books of history written in that time.

During all these four hundred years most of the Jews were living in the land of Palestine—waiting. The Jews had been waiting since the time of the great prophet Isaiah, who lived seven hundred years earlier. They had been waiting and longing since the time of their first forefather, Abraham, who lived nineteen hundred years before.

For what were the Jewish people waiting and longing?

They were waiting for a child, whom God had promised to send to some Jewish mother.

God first gave this promise to Eve, when He said that some day one of her children would overcome Satan, who had brought sin and death into the world by tempting Eve to disobey God. This wonderful child who was to come would again bring goodness and everlasting life to man.

Many years later, God promised Abraham that this child would be one of his descendants, and that all the nations of the earth would be blessed in him. Nineteen hundred years had passed since that time, but during all those centuries the Jewish people had been looking for that child.

The great prophet Isaiah, who lived seven hundred years before the time when the child was to be born, foretold his coming in these words: "Unto us a child is born, unto us a son is given; and the government shall be upon his shoulder; and his name shall be called Wonderful, Counselor, the mighty God, the everlasting Father, the Prince of Peace."

The prophet Micah had even foretold that this wonderful child would be born in the city of Bethlehem.

Besides these, God had made many other promises about the child whom He would send. No wonder that every Jewish mother wished to have a little son! No wonder she hoped, deep in her heart that the long-promised child would come to her!

At last the time came when the child was to be born. God sent a messenger to announce his coming.

There was in the land of Israel, a very good old priest named Zacharias. His wife was named Elisabeth. When all the people came to the Temple to pray and to worship God, it was Zacharias' work to go into the Temple and burn sweet-smelling incense on the altar.

This good old priest and his wife had one sorrow. They had no child, and they were now so old that they could no longer expect that one would come to them.

One day while Zacharias was burning incense on the altar, he looked up. There on the right side of the altar stood a bright and glorious angel!

Zacharias was very much frightened. The angel spoke kindly to him, telling him not to be afraid. God had heard his prayer. He was going to give Zacharias and Elisabeth a son, who must be called John. Many people would be glad at the child's birth, for John was to make the people ready for that blessed child who had been promised so long.

Zacharias was amazed. He asked, "How shall I know that what you have said will come true? I am an old man, and my wife is old, too."

The angel replied, "I am the great angel Gabriel that stands in God's holy presence. It was God who sent me to tell you this glad news. But because you have not believed my message, you shall be unable to speak until the child is born."

While the angel was talking to Zacharias, the people outside were wondering what had delayed the priest so long in the Temple. Finally Zacharias came outside. He had to beckon to the people with his hand, for he could not speak.

In a few days Zacharias was through with his work in the Temple, and he returned home. When Elisabeth knew that God was going to give her a son in her old age, she was very happy.

CHAPTER 2

The Message of the Angel

LUKE 1

In the city of Nazareth there lived a cousin of Elisabeth, a sweet and good young girl named Mary. She was not yet married, but she soon would be, for she had promised a good man, Joseph, that she would become his wife.

One day when Mary was alone, the angel Gabriel appeared to her with a joyful message. God was pleased with Mary. He would give her the greatest honor that any woman has ever had. God would send her a son, who would also be a son of the most high God, a king who would reign forever. This was the child who had been promised to Eve and to Abraham. This was the child for whom all the Jews had been waiting.

Mary asked, "But how can I have a child when I am not married?"

Then the angel told Mary that her son would not have any earthly father. He would be the Son of God Himself. And since he was to be the son of God and of Mary, he would himself be both God and man.

Mary said humbly, "Behold, the handmaid of the Lord; be it unto me according to your word."

Mary was so full of joy that she did not know how to contain it. She could not keep this news to herself! She felt that she must tell someone.

The angel had told Mary that Elisabeth her cousin also was to have a son. So Mary made herself ready and went into the hill country to pay a visit to Elisabeth.

As soon as Mary spoke to her, Elisabeth called out in a loud voice, "Oh, you are a blessed woman! And you will have a blessed child! It is a great honor that the mother of my Lord should come to see me."

Mary answered, "I am filled with love and praise for God. He has given me the greatest of honors. Although I am only a poor girl, the whole world till the end of time will call me blessed."

Mary and Elisabeth were so happy as they talked to each other about what God had done for them, that they could not bear to be separated. Mary stayed with Elisabeth for three months. Then she went back to her own home. She must begin making little baby-clothes, to be ready for her precious son. She must tell Joseph about the wonderful thing that had happened to her.

Joseph had not seen the angel who told Mary that she was to be the mother of the long-promised Savior. He did not understand how such a thing could be. He began to think that it might be better if he did not marry her.

While Joseph was thinking and wondering, he had a remarkable dream one night. In this dream an angel appeared to him saying that he should take Mary for his wife. Her child would be the son of God. The child must be named Jesus, which means *Savior*, for he would save his people from their sins. When Joseph awakened he did not forget his dream. He took Mary for his wife as the angel had commanded.

Not long after this, Elisabeth's baby was born. When the child was eight days old, the friends and relatives of the family came to Elisabeth's house to give the baby a name, as was the custom among the Jews.

These people wanted to call the child Zacharias, after his father. Elisabeth said firmly, "No, we are not going to call him Zacharias. His name is to be John."

The friends thought that such talk was very strange. "But none of your family is named John," they said. The old priest was still unable to speak, but they made signs to him, to see what he wanted to call his son.

Zacharias asked for a writing tablet. On it he wrote, "His name is John."

While the friends were wondering at this, all at once Zacharias was able to speak again. First of all he praised God for His goodness, because He was going to send the long-promised child into the world. Then Zacharias turned to his little son and said, "And thou, child, shalt be called the prophet of the Most High, for thou shalt go before the face of the Lord to make ready His ways."

Little John grew up to be a boy of strong and noble spirit. He loved to be alone, so that he could think about God. When he became a young man he went to live in the desert so that he could prepare himself for his work to announce the coming of God's son into the world.

CHAPTER 3

The Holy Night

LUKE 2

It happened, in those days, that the Roman emperor Caesar Augustus, who ruled over most of the world, made a law that all the people in his kingdom should pay a tax to the Roman government. He ordered everyone to go to his native city and to stay there till the tax officers came around to tell each man how much money he must pay.

Joseph and Mary had to travel to the little town of Bethlehem near Jerusalem to be taxed. They lived in Nazareth, but Joseph had descended from the family of David; and David had lived in Bethlehem.

Bethlehem was a little town. It was crowded at this time, for many people belonging to the family of David had come to be taxed. By the time Joseph and Mary reached the town, every house was full of visitors. No one had room for them. What were they to do? They surely could not stay in the street!

There was only one place where they found a welcome. That was a stable where animals were sheltered. Here Mary and Joseph found a bed of soft sweet hay.

That night was a blessed night, and that lowly stable became a holy place. For on that night, the Savior of the world was born. God sent His own son into the world to be Mary's baby.

How happy Mary was, now that she held the promised child in her arms! Her heart was filled with love and adoration. This tiny child was her own baby, but he was also the Son of the great and mighty God! Mary looked at him tenderly and adoringly, for she knew that this tiny child was to be the Savior of the world. She put some soft hay in the manger out of which the cattle ate, and laid the baby Jesus on the hay.

When a prince is born on earth, all the bells throughout the kingdom are rung for joy. Heralds and trumpeters ride in every direction to proclaim the birth of the king's son. So too, when God's Son was born on earth, heralds came to announce his coming. They were not men riding on horses, blowing trumpets of brass. They were glorious angels, bright and shining.

On the night when Jesus was born, there were shepherds in the fields near Bethlehem, keeping watch over their flocks by night. Suddenly the glory of the Lord shone round about them. A light from Heaven, more glorious than the light of the sun, filled the sky. An angel of the Lord came near them, and they were very much afraid.

The angel said, "Be not afraid, for behold, I bring you good tidings of great joy, which shall be to all the people. For unto you is born this day in the city of David a Savior, which is Christ the Lord. And this is the sign unto you. You shall find the babe wrapped in swaddling clothes and lying in a manger."

Suddenly the sky was filled with angels, praising God and saying, "Glory to God in the highest, and on earth peace among men in whom He is well pleased."

The glory of God was shining over all the earth, as if heaven itself were opened, and the shepherds were gazing into it. They forgot their flocks as they gazed at the dazzling glory and listened to the wonderful words. How radiant the light! How glorious the angels! What marvelous music!

No king's son was ever announced so splendidly! The angels sang with joy that the Savior was born, who would save his people from their sins and from death.

After the angels had gone back into Heaven, the shepherds said one to another, "Let us now go to Bethlehem to see this strange thing which the Lord has made known to us." As fast as they could, they ran to Bethlehem. There, in a stable, they found Joseph and Mary, and the baby lying in a manger. The shepherds knew that this was the child who had been promised to their fathers for so many hundreds of years. They kneeled down in adoration before him.

As they went back to their sheep, they were so filled with the wonder of what they had seen and heard that they glorified and praised God. They stopped every one whom they met to tell about the glorious angels and their message.

Now when the baby was eight days old, he was given the name Jesus, as the angel had commanded. This name means *Savior*.

It was a custom among the Jews that on the day a baby boy was a month old he was brought to the Temple and presented to the Lord. Therefore a month after the baby Jesus was born, Mary and Joseph brought him to Jerusalem.

In this city there was a very good old man named Simeon. He was one of those who had been looking and longing most earnestly for the long-promised child to be born. God had spoken to him and told him that before his death he would see the Christ-child.

Just at the time when Joseph and Mary brought the child Jesus to the Temple, God's spirit led Simeon there. The good old man knew at once that this was the Christ-child. He took the baby in his arms, and looking up to heaven he said, "Now, Lord, I am ready to die, for now I have seen the promised child who is to be the Savior of the world and the glory of Thy people Israel."

In the Temple there was also a very old lady who spent most of her time there praying to God. She too saw the baby and knew that he was the long-promised Savior. She carried the glad news to all the people in Jerusalem who had been looking for his coming.

CHAPTER 4

A Star in the East

MATTHEW 2

Although the baby Jesus was now more than a month old, Mary and Joseph had not yet gone back to their own city of Nazareth. Perhaps the taxing was not finished, or perhaps they thought the baby was too young to travel. While they were still in Bethlehem, a very strange thing happened.

In ancient days, there were wise men in some of the eastern lands who used to study the stars at night. They did not know so much about the stars as we do, because they did not have telescopes; but still they did learn many things about the sky. They knew where to find many of the bright stars which they studied night after night. They came to know a great deal about the movement of the stars.

Far to the east of the land of the Jews, some of these wise men were living. Perhaps the country in which they lived was Persia, for in that climate the stars are very bright and easy to watch.

One night, while these wise men were gazing into the sky, they saw a new star, an unusually bright one. This discovery excited them. As they watched the star, it moved. They were still more surprised. What could this mean?

In those days men believed that such a bright new star had special meaning. Perhaps it meant that a child was born who would become a great king or a wise general. So they watched this strangely moving star, and they decided that it must have been sent to announce the birth of a great king.

So firmly did the wise men believe this that they started out to find the prince whose coming was foretold by the star. With them they took rich gifts for the baby king. They made the journey with camels, for most of the way led through deserts. During the hot day the wise men slept. They travelled in the cool night when they could follow the star.

At last the wise men rode into the streets of Jerusalem on their camels. The people of the city gazed curiously at these important-looking strangers. Who could they be? Where had they come from?

Soon the strangers stopped. They called out to some of the passers-by, "Where is the child that is born King of the Jews? We have seen his star in the east, and we have come to worship him."

A crowd gathered around, to hear what the travellers were asking. The word was passed around, "These men say that a king of the Jews has been born. Where is he? We have not heard of any king."

One of the crowd hurried into King Herod's palace and said, "Some foreign-looking men rode into Jerusalem today on their camels. They are asking everybody, 'Where is the child who is born to be king of the Jews?' They say that they saw his star in the east, and that they are come to worship him!"

King Herod was disturbed. Was it possible that some child had been born who was going to be king of the Jews instead of Herod and his family? He called all the chief priests and scribes, and asked, "Tell me, where do the Scriptures say that the Christ is to be born?"

The priests and scribes knew about the old prophecy, for they spent all their time studying the Scriptures. They said to the king, "He is to be born in Bethlehem, because it was written by the prophet, 'And thou, Bethlehem, in the land of Judah, out of thee shall come forth a governor who shall be shepherd of my people Israel.'"

Hearing this, King Herod sent some one to tell the strangers to come to him. He asked them exactly when they had seen the star. "Go to Bethlehem," he said. "Look there for the child. When you have found him, come back and tell me all about him, for I, too, would like to come and worship him."

Of course, Herod had not the slightest intention of worshipping the new-born king, for he was a wicked and cruel man. He meant to kill the baby as soon as he found out where he was, so that the child could not grow up and become a king.

The wise men left the palace and started out for Bethlehem, which was only a few miles away. It was night. To their joy they saw the star shining in the sky above them!

The star was moving. The wise men were sure that it had been sent to guide them to the place where the child was. They followed it till they came to Bethlehem. At the very place where the young child was, the star stood still.

The wise men went into the house. There they saw the little child whose star they had followed so far, and they kneeled down and worshipped him. Opening their treasures, they took out the precious gifts which they had brought — gold and rare perfumes called frankincense and myrrh.

The wise men had found the child they were looking for, but they did not go back and tell Herod all about him. God, who was taking care of His son all the time, sent a dream warning the wise men not to go back to Herod. They went home to their own country by another way, and Herod waited for them in vain.

CHAPTER 5

Warned By a Dream

MATTHEW 2

After the wise men had gone back to their own country, God sent an angel to Joseph in a dream, saying, "Get ready quickly, take the baby and his mother, and go away from here at once. Hurry far away into the land of Egypt, and stay there till I tell you to come back again. Herod will try to find the baby in order to kill him."

Then Joseph rose up from his sleep, and wakened Mary. "God has sent me a dream," he told her. "An angel spoke to me, and told me that Herod was going to try to kill the baby. We must hurry down into Egypt and stay there till he brings us word to come back. Hurry and get ready. We must go at once, so as to get far away before the morning light comes."

Mary dressed herself as fast as she could. She wrapped some clothes together in a bundle, while Joseph hurried to find a donkey for Mary to ride on. Very soon they were ready to start.

Mary wrapped her precious child up warmly, holding him in her arms as she rode on the donkey. Without telling anybody, they slipped away in the darkness. They rode all night, and when the daylight came they were many miles away.

And it was a good thing that they were far away. When Herod discovered that the wise men had gone home without coming back to tell him about the child, he was furiously angry. He was the more determined to kill the baby who was to become king.

This is what King Herod did. He sent his soldiers to Bethlehem with orders to kill every baby boy in the whole town, from the little new-born babies to those that were two years old. "Now," thought the wicked king, "the baby whose star the wise men saw will surely be killed."

Herod could not kill God's son! Jesus was safe in Egypt. He was lying in his mother's arms under the shade of a waving palm tree, and the warm Egyptian sun was smiling down upon them.

But what a scene of terror in Bethlehem! The soldiers went into every house, killing every baby boy they found. In vain the mothers tried to save their children. In vain they cried. They could not be comforted.

Not long afterwards, **wicked** Herod died. When Herod was dead, an angel of the Lord appeared again in a dream to Joseph in Egypt, and said to him, "Arise and take the young child and his mother, and go into the land of Israel."

So Joseph took Jesus and Mary back to the land of Israel. When he heard that Herod's son was now king, he was afraid to go near the city of Jerusalem, where the king lived. Instead, he went to Nazareth, which was far away from Jerusalem. There little Jesus grew up. Joseph was a carpenter, and the people of Nazareth must often have seen the boy Jesus helping Joseph in his shop.

CHAPTER 6

The Boy in the Temple

LUKE 2

Jesus lived in the little town of Nazareth. As he grew older he became a fine, tall boy. The other boys often listened to him, because he was wiser than they were. They admired him and loved him, because he was good.

Although Jesus was a boy like other boys, in one thing he was very different from any other person who has ever lived. His heart was good — perfectly good. He never did anything wrong. He never even had any wrong thoughts or desires. He could not sin, for he was the blessed Son of God.

All other children, since the time when Adam and Eve sinned against God by eating the forbidden fruit, have been born with bad hearts. Jesus was one of Eve's children, but he was also the Son of the good God, and he did not inherit the sinful nature of his human mother. He was perfectly good throughout his whole life.

Even as a small child, Jesus showed how much he loved God. When he became twelve years old he was very happy, for at that age Jewish boys were allowed to go to Jerusalem with their parents to join in the celebration of the Passover Feast which was held there every year.

Nazareth was sixty miles from Jerusalem — a great distance in those days. At the time of the Passover many people from Nazareth went down to Jerusalem together, so that Jesus and Mary and Joseph did not travel alone. As they passed through cities and villages on their way, many others joined the people from Nazareth. There came to be a great procession of people on their way to keep the feast.

Some of the people in the procession walked, while others rode on donkeys. At noon they all sat down by the wayside to eat their

simple meal. At night they spread rugs on the ground and slept together under the open sky.

After several days of travelling, the company from Nazareth
reached Jerusalem. For seven days they celebrated the Feast of the
Passover. At the end of the week they started for home again.

Since so many friends and neighbors were travelling together,
Joseph and Mary did not notice that Jesus was not with them. When
they did miss him, they did not worry. They thought, "He is surely
somewhere in the company. Probably he is walking along with some
of his friends."

For a whole day Joseph and Mary went on without Jesus. As
they went along, they asked here and there among their friends, "Have
you seen our son, Jesus?"

The answer was always, "No, we have not seen him. He has not
been with us at all."

Joseph and Mary inquired of everyone but could find no trace of
Jesus. At last they became alarmed. Was their precious boy lost? What
could have happened to him?

There was nothing to do but to return to Jerusalem. They had a
whole day's walk back to the city. They inquired of everyone they met
on the way, "Have you seen anything of our son? He is twelve years
old, a fine, tall, strong boy." Always the answer was the same. No one
had seen anything of Jesus.

When Joseph and Mary reached Jerusalem, they walked the
streets of the big city for two days, without finding a trace of Jesus.
At last they looked for him in the Temple, and there they found him.
He was sitting in the midst of very learned men, called doctors of
the law. He was listening to their learned talk, and he was asking them
questions that they could not answer.

All the teachers were amazed to think that a twelve year old boy
could give such wise answers to the questions they asked him, and could
ask them questions which were so hard to answer.

Joseph and Mary were astonished to see Jesus talking to the
learned men. Yet they could not forget how anxious they had been.

His mother said to him, "Son, why have you done this? Your father and I have been looking everywhere for you and have been very sorrowful that we could not find you."

Jesus answered, "Why did you look for me? Didn't you know that I must begin to do my Father's business?"

Jesus meant that he must begin to do the work of his Heavenly Father. But Joseph and Mary did not understand this answer. They did not know that he meant that there was work he must do for God.

Jesus went back to Nazareth with his parents. But Mary kept all these sayings in her heart and wondered about them.

CHAPTER 7

The Preacher in the Desert

Matthew 3; Mark 1; Luke 3

In the little town of Nazareth Jesus lived quietly with his parents. There he grew into manhood. Probably he helped Joseph in the carpenter shop. Often he prayed to his Father in Heaven.

Meanwhile, John, the son of Zacharias and Elisabeth, had gone to live in the wilderness. It was lonely there, but John wanted to be apart from people so that he might have time to think about God.

God took good care of John, for there was a great work for John to do. He was to preach to the people and make them ready to listen to Jesus, who would soon begin to teach.

John lived a rough life in the desert. He ate locusts, as the people of the desert still do. There was plenty of honey which wild bees stored away in holes in the rocks. John was dressed in a loose, rough shirt made of camel's hair, with a leather girdle around his waist.

While John was living in the desert, both he and Jesus became about thirty years old. It was time for them to begin the work that they had been born to do. The word of God came to John in the wilderness, telling him to go and preach to the people, to prepare their minds for Jesus.

Gradually the people of Jerusalem and throughout the land of Judea learned that there was a man preaching in the desert, near the Jordan River. He was strange and wild looking, dressed in rough camel's hair, wearing a leather girdle about his waist.

"Who is he?" they asked. "Where did he come from?"

Nobody knew.

"For a long time he has lived in the desert," people said. "He is a holy man, a prophet."

Great crowds came out to hear John preach to them. And what was this strange man saying? He was telling the people how sinful and wicked they were. He was crying out to them that they must turn away from their sins and be baptized, for the kingdom of heaven was coming.

When John warned the people to turn away from their sins, many of them were struck to the heart at the thought of their own wickedness. They came to John and said, "We are sorry for our sins, and we want to live better lives. Will you baptize us?"

Many who had been living sinful lives were turned back to the Lord through this strange new preacher. People began to ask, "Is it possible that John is the long-expected Christ? Or can he be the prophet Elijah come to life again?"

At last some of the Jews at Jerusalem sent several priests and Levites down to the Jordan where John was baptizing, to find out the truth. They came to John and asked, "Who are you? Are you the Christ whom we have been expecting so long?"

"No," said John, "I am not the Christ."

"Are you Elijah?"

"No," said John, "I am not Elijah."

"Then who are you?" asked the priests. "We have been sent to find out."

"I am the voice of one crying in the wilderness, 'Make ye ready the way of the Lord,'" said John. Then he went on to tell them that after him would come someone so much greater than he, that John would not be worthy to stoop down to untie his shoe. It was Jesus of whom he spoke.

The next day, as John was preaching, he saw Jesus himself coming among the people to be baptized. After Jesus had been baptized, he came up out of the water praying. The heavens were opened, and the Holy Spirit came down out of Heaven in the shape of a dove, and alighted upon Jesus. At the same moment a voice came out of Heaven saying, "Thou art My beloved son; in thee I am well pleased."

How surprised the people must have been! They looked at Jesus in awe. Many of them had been thinking that John was the expected Messiah, even after he had said, "I am come to prepare the way for the Christ."

Knowing their amazement, John said, "See! This is the Lamb of God, who takes away the sin of the world. This is the one I told you of, when I said, 'After me comes one who is greater than I.' I myself did not know who it would be, but God said to me, 'I will send My spirit upon him in the form of a dove, and it will remain on him. That is the one who is My son.' Now I have seen, and have told you that this Jesus is the Son of God."

When the people went home that night they could talk only of the strange things which they had seen and heard that day. Those who had been looking and longing for the Christ to come—how happy they must have been that night!

CHAPTER 8

Satan Talks to God's Son

MATTHEW 4; MARK 1; LUKE 4

After Jesus had been baptized, the Spirit of God led him into the wild and lonely wilderness, where only wild beasts made their homes. For forty days and forty nights Jesus stayed there. During all that time he had nothing to eat, and he became very hungry. While he was there, the devil came to him and tried to make him do something wrong.

Satan knew that Jesus was perfectly good, and that he was the Son of God, as well as the son of Mary. Satan knew, too, that Jesus had come into the world to save people from sin and death, which had come into the world when Satan tempted Eve to disobey God. Now Satan was going to try to tempt Jesus to do wrong, also.

At the end of the forty days, Jesus was very hungry, for during all that time he had eaten nothing. Knowing this, the devil whispered slyly, "If you are God's son, turn this stone into bread to satisfy your hunger."

Jesus answered, "God has told us that man needs more than bread to live. Man needs every word that God has spoken."

Satan tried again. This time he took Jesus into Jerusalem and set him upon a pinnacle of the Temple. Then he said, "Throw yourself down to the ground, if you are God's son, for it is written in the Bible, 'He shall give His angels charge over thee, and in their hands they shall bear thee up, lest thou dash thy foot against a stone.' "

But Jesus answered, "It is also written in the Bible, 'Thou shalt not make trial of the Lord thy God.' "

Still Satan did not give up. He took Jesus up to the top of a very high mountain. In a moment of time he showed Jesus all the kingdoms of the world and the glory of them.

Then he said to Jesus, 'All this power and glory belongs to me, and I can give it to whomsoever I will. If you will fall down and worship me, I will give it to you."

But Jesus had come into the world to conquer the devil, not to worship him. So he said, "Get thee behind me, Satan. It is written in the Bible, 'Thou shalt worship the Lord thy God, and Him only shalt thou serve.' "

The devil saw that Jesus resisted all his temptations. For a time he left Jesus alone.

Jesus was conqueror, but he was tired and worn out and almost starved with hunger. Angels came down from Heaven, to take care of the weak and starving Jesus. They gave him all that he needed, and soon he was rested.

CHAPTER 9

Jesus Chooses His Disciples

JOHN 1

One day as John and two of his disciples were standing together, Jesus walked past them. John said, "Behold, the Lamb of God!"

The two disciples who were with John could not bear to lose sight of this stranger whom John called "the Lamb of God." They left their master standing there and followed Jesus at a distance. Jesus turned and saw them following. "What are you looking for?" he asked.

They said, "Master, where do you live?"

"Come with me, and see," answered Jesus.

So the two men came to the place where Jesus was staying, and they remained with him for several hours. How happy they were to listen to his wonderful words! They became his followers.

One of the two men who visited Jesus that day was named Andrew. The first thing Andrew did, after spending the afternoon with Jesus, was to find his brother Simon. He said to him, "Simon, I have a wonderful thing to tell you. We have found the long-expected Messiah!"

Simon went with Andrew to talk with Jesus, and he too became one of Jesus' firmest friends. Jesus gave Simon a new name which fitted him very well—the name "Peter," which means "a rock."

The next day, Jesus found a man named Philip, whom he wanted to be one of his disciples. He said to Philip, "Follow me."

Philip went with Jesus gladly. He wanted his friend Nathanael to know about the teacher whom he was following. He looked for Nathanael and told him, "We have found the long-expected one about whom Moses and the prophets wrote. His name is Jesus of Nazareth."

Of course Nathanael could hardly believe this news. The Jews did not expect the Messiah to come from Nazareth. The prophets had said that he would be born in Bethlehem. Nathanael did not know the story of Jesus' birth in the stable of Bethlehem.

"Come with me and see a man. . . ." John 4

. . . for he could see ! John 7

"Come and see," Philip urged. So the two friends set out.

As Jesus saw Nathanael coming towards him he said, "There is a truly good man."

"How do you know what kind of man I am?" asked Nathanael in surprise.

Jesus said, "Before Philip called you, when you were under the fig tree, I saw you, and I knew then what kind of man you were."

Nathanael saw that Jesus must be divine, for he knew things that no man could know. He opened his heart to Jesus. "Master, you are the Son of God, you are the King of Israel," he said.

"Is it only because I said I saw you under the fig tree, that you believe on me?" asked Jesus. "You shall see greater things than these. You shall see the heaven opened, and the angels of God coming down to the Son of man."

In this way Jesus gathered a little group of friends or disciples. They followed him wherever he went, listening to his teaching.

CHAPTER 10

Jesus at the Wedding Feast

John 2

A few miles from Nazareth was a little town called Cana. The people of the two villages probably visited each other often, since they lived so near each other. Their children played together in the fields, and every year the people walked together down the road to Jerusalem to celebrate the Passover.

In this village lived some friends of Mary, the mother of Jesus. A few days after Jesus met his first followers, these people in Cana invited Mary and Jesus and his friends to a wedding party.

It was the custom of the Jews to celebrate a wedding by holding a feast. Sometimes the party lasted for two or three days. The guests had a good time, talking and eating and drinking.

Many people besides Jesus and his friends went to the wedding in Cana — more people than had been prepared for. Before the feast was over, the servants discovered that there was not enough wine for all the guests. They were dismayed.

Mary discovered the trouble. She knew that her son had great power. She did not ask him to help; but she went to him and said simply, "They have no wine." To the servants she said, "Whatever he tells you, do it." She believed that Jesus would help them.

Near at hand there were six stone jars, each one almost as large as a barrel. In these jars water was kept for the household, for the Jews washed their hands and feet before eating. Jesus told the servants to fill these jars up to the brim with fresh water. When they had done it he said, "Pour some of it out, and take it to the ruler of the feast."

The servants had filled the jars with water. What they drew out was not water, but fragrant, miraculous wine. Can you imagine how awed they must have felt when they saw this marvelous thing?

The man who was chosen to be ruler of the feast had to taste the food before it was served to the other guests. The servants brought him some of the new wine, but they did not tell him what had happened or where it had come from. When he had tasted it, the man called the young man who was giving the feast and said, "Usually people serve the best wine first, and when people have drunk freely they set out poorer wine; but you have kept the best until now."

This miracle was a sign of the wonderful power which Jesus had, and which he used to help others. It was the first time people knew that Jesus could do things which no man could do. Seeing it, his disciples remembered what Jesus had said to Nathanael: "You shall see greater things than these." And they believed on him.

CHAPTER 11

The Father's House

JOHN 2

Soon after Jesus took Peter and the other men to be his followers, they travelled together towards the city of Jerusalem. It was the time of year when the Feast of the Passover was held, and from all parts of the land people began to stream to Jerusalem.

For many, many years the Jews had held this feast in memory of that terrible night when Israel fled out of Egypt. On that night the Angel of Death killed every first-born among the Egyptians, but passed over the houses of the Israelites which were sprinkled with the blood of a lamb. In gratitude, every Jew twelve years or older kept the feast in Jerusalem for one week every year.

With all the rest of the people, Jesus and his followers went to the feast. Jesus was eager to visit the Temple, his Father's house. But in the court of the Temple he found noisy confusion. The place was crowded with men selling oxen and sheep and doves to be used as sacrifices. At other tables men were changing foreign money into the kind of coins which the Jews gave to the Temple. The noises of the animals and the ring of coins mingled with the bargaining of the men who bought and sold. The Temple looked like a market, instead of a holy place where God was worshipped.

Jesus made a whip out of cords, and drove the sellers and their animals out of the Temple. He overturned the tables of the money changers, and told the dove-sellers to take their doves some other place.

Some of the Jews did not like Jesus to take so much authority. They asked him to prove that he had a right to do this. Jesus said, "Destroy this temple, and in three days I will raise it up."

The Jews thought he meant that he could build, in three days, the splendid Temple in Jerusalem which had taken forty-six years to build. By the word "temple" Jesus had meant his body, which would be crucified by the Jews and which he would make alive again in three days. Even the disciples did not understand what Jesus meant, but they trusted him.

Many others who saw Jesus and heard his teaching came to believe on him. They saw him heal sick people just by laying his hands on them, or by speaking; and they knew he told the truth when he said he was the Son of God. Those who truly believed were baptized by the disciples.

Some of the people who began to follow Jesus had been baptized by John, who was still preaching and baptizing near the Jordan River. John's disciples came to him and said, "Teacher, the man whom you called 'the Lamb of God' is now baptizing people. Many are leaving us and are listening to him."

John replied, "I told you that I am not the Christ, but am sent before him. I am full of joy that he has come. I am from the earth, but he is from heaven. God sent him and he speaks the words of God. God the Father loves him. He who believes on the Son of God shall have everlasting life. He who does not believe on him shall not have everlasting life but God will be angry with him forever."

CHAPTER 12

A Visit by Night

JOHN 3

Now I shall tell you something very hard to understand:

Before Jesus was born as a little baby in Bethlehem, he was with God in Heaven. *He himself was God.* Jesus always has been God, even from eternity. He is God the Son.

We know that there is only one God. But that God is three persons—three separate and equal persons—God the Father, God the Son, and God the Holy Spirit. Before Jesus came to earth as Mary's son, to die for our sins, he was already God the Son. He lived in Heaven with God the Father and God the Holy Spirit. The Father created the heavens and the earth. The Holy Spirit lives in our hearts today and makes us love the right. The Son, Jesus, died for our sins. These three are one God, and have lived from all eternity. We know this is true, because Jesus told us.

This Jesus who walked about on earth was truly God. He went about healing the sick, and preaching. And the people loved him. They listened eagerly to his preaching.

Among those who listened to Jesus was a man named Nicodemus. Nicodemus was a ruler of the Jews, a Pharisee. The Pharisees were men who kept all the laws of Moses very strictly; and they kept many other rules besides, which they themselves had made. They were proud of their strictness, and thought themselves better than other people, even better than Jesus. They would not listen to Jesus.

But Nicodemus was not like the other Pharisees. He heard Jesus teach, and saw the miracles, and he wondered what kind of man this Jesus might be. Nicodemus did not quite dare to speak to Jesus openly, for fear the other Pharisees would scorn him. But he did want to know more about this teacher who talked so much about God and the Kingdom of God.

So Nicodemus went to Jesus one night. He said to Jesus, "Teacher, we know that God sent you, for no one could do these miracles that you do unless God were with him."

Jesus said to him, "No one can see the Kingdom of God unless he is born again."

That was a strange answer. Nicodemus did not understand. Surely, he would like to see the Kingdom of God. But he was a grown man. Must he be born again? Must he be a baby again?

Jesus said, "Verily, verily, except one be born of water and the Spirit, he cannot enter the Kingdom of God."

Then Jesus went on to explain. Not one of us can be a child of God without a new heart. Jesus made that very strong when he said, "Verily, verily . . ." But if we believe on Him, the Holy Spirit gives us a new heart. We are "born again." We become children of God.

We cannot understand how the Holy Spirit gives us a new heart, just as we cannot understand how the wind blows. But the Bible tells us, "For God so loved the world that He gave His only begotten Son, that whosoever believeth on him should not perish, but have everlasting life." We must believe on Jesus to be born again.

Nicodemus was a good man. He kept the law of God carefully. But that was not enough to open the way into the Kingdom of God. Being good does not get us into the Kingdom of God at all. Unless the Holy Spirit gives us a new heart, we cannot see the Kingdom of God.

Nicodemus listened carefully. He had never heard such wonderful words. He could not understand. But when he went away he thought and thought about it. And after a while he did believe in Jesus. He was born again, and he became a child of God.

CHAPTER 13

The Woman at Jacob's Well

JOHN 4

After a time Jesus left Judea and went towards Nazareth, the city in Galilee in which he had grown up. This was a distance of more than sixty miles.

As Jesus and his disciples walked along, they came to a city of Samaria in which there was a very old well, made long ago by Jacob.

In that hot country water is very precious. There was usually only one well in a whole village. Every day the people brought their pitchers there and drew as much water as they needed.

The well of Jacob probably had a low stone wall around the top to keep people from falling in. This stone coping made a good seat. Very likely a few palm-trees grew over it and made the spot shady.

As Jesus was very tired from the journey, he sat down by Jacob's well to rest himself. It was noon-day. The disciples went to the village to buy some food.

While Jesus was sitting there a woman of Samaria came to the well to draw water. Jesus was hot and thirsty, as well as tired. He asked the Samaritan woman to give him a drink of her water.

The woman looked surprised that Jesus, who was a Jew, should ask a drink of her, a Samaritan. The Jews hated the Samaritans and would have nothing to do with them, because the Samaritans knew very little about the true God.

The woman asked, "How is it that you are willing to ask a drink of me, a Samaritan woman?"

Jesus said, "If you knew who I am, you would ask me to give you living water."

The woman said, "Sir, the well is deep, and you have no pitcher to let down into it. How then can you get that 'living water'?"

"Whoever drinks this water will be thirsty again," replied Jesus. "But whoever drinks the water that I shall give him will never be thirsty again, for the water that I shall give him will be in him a well of water, springing up unto eternal life."

Jesus was not speaking of water which one drinks. He meant that he would put his Spirit into her heart, and that her soul would be refreshed by his Spirit as her body was by water.

The woman did not understand this. She said, "Sir, give me this water, so that I will not be thirsty, nor have to come here to draw water."

To make the woman realize that he was not an ordinary man, Jesus told her many things about her life. She was startled. How could this man tell her all about her past life? He had never seen her before! She said to him, "Sir, I see that you are a prophet."

Then she asked him something which had often troubled her. "Our fathers," she said, "always worshipped in this mountain; but you Jews say that in Jerusalem is the place where men ought to worship. Which is right?"

Now, Jesus was always teaching the people about his Heavenly Father. When the Samaritan woman asked this question, Jesus answered it in such a way that he taught her more about God than she had ever known.

"God does not command us to worship Him in any special place," he said, "It is in our hearts that we must worship Him. God is a Spirit, and they that worship Him must worship Him in spirit and in truth."

Once more the woman realized that she was talking with a remarkable person. She said, "I know that Christ is coming, and when he comes he will tell us the truth about everything." Even this Samaritan woman, who knew little about the true God, was longing for the promised Savior.

Jesus said to her, "I am the Christ."

The woman could not keep this splendid news to herself. In her excitement she left her water jar by the well and hurried into the city. "Come with me and see a man who told me everything that I did in my whole life," she called to the people she met. "Don't you think that he must be the Christ?"

The men were stirred by her excitement. Many of them went with her to the well to see for themselves. Some of them believed on Jesus because of what the woman had said. They begged him to stay with them, so that they might see his miracles and hear his words of life.

For two days Jesus stayed with the Samaritans. Many accepted him as the Christ. No longer did they believe only because of what the woman told them. After they heard him, they knew truly that this was the Christ, the Savior of the world.

CHAPTER 14

The Father Who Believed

JOHN 4

Everywhere Jesus went, the people were eager to hear his blessed. words. The disciples had received him gladly, without hesitation. So had many of the Jews in Jerusalem, who saw his miracles. Even the Pharisee Nicodemus had said, "We know that you are a teacher come from God."

When Jesus passed through the land of Samaria many more people believed on him as they saw his works of healing. "The long-expected Messiah has come," said the people, and they were filled with joy.

After Jesus had stayed two days with the Samaritans, he continued his journey into Galilee. The people of the country were very glad to have Jesus come to them. They too had kept the Feast of the Passover in Jerusalem, and had seen all the miracles which Jesus did there. They wanted to know more about this teacher. The sick and the lame and the blind hoped that he would heal them.

In Capernaum, which was a large city of Galilee, there lived a nobleman whose son was very ill. The poor father had almost given up hope that the boy would live, and his heart was sad. If only his son would get well, he would be happy.

This father had heard of the miracles which Jesus did. He knew about the water turned into wine at the wedding in Cana, which was only twenty miles from his home. He had heard of the people whom Jesus healed at the feast in Jerusalem. The news that Jesus had come into Galilee and was staying at Cana gave him hope. Could he possibly get this wonderful healer to come and see his son? Perhaps his boy, too, might be made well again!

The anxious father hurried to Cana. He found the Master and told him about the sick boy. He begged Jesus to come and cure his son.

Jesus did not go down to Capernaum. He could cure the sick boy without going to see him. He said to the father, "Go back home, for your son is living."

The man believed that Jesus was able to heal his son. He turned home again, happy and confident. On the way, his servants met him with the joyful news that the boy was much better, and that his fever was completely gone.

"When did he begin to get better?" asked the father.

The servants said, "The fever left him yesterday at one o'clock." Gratefully the father remembered that at that very hour Jesus had said, "Your son will live."

It was a happy household once more that night. The thankful father knew that his dear son had been given back to him from the very door of death. He and all his family believed in Jesus, for they had seen his power.

CHAPTER 15

The Mob That Wanted a Miracle

LUKE 4

At last Jesus came to his own city, Nazareth, where he had grown up. His mother and brothers and his childhood friends still lived there. They must have been eager to see him again, for since the Passover feast in Jerusalem everyone had been talking about the miracles Jesus did there.

It was Jesus' custom, wherever he happened to be on the Sabbath day, to go into the synagogue, as the Jews called their church. He often read parts of the Bible to the people and explained the meaning. And so on the Sabbath day which Jesus spent in Nazareth, he went as usual to the synagogue and stood up to read to the people.

In those days the Bible was not printed in one book of many pages, as it is today. It was written on long strips, each book rolled up separately. One of these rolls—the roll of the prophet Isaiah—was given to Jesus to read from.

Isaiah had lived hundreds of years before the birth of Jesus, but God had told him about many things that would come to pass after his death. Many times Isaiah had prophesied about the Messiah whom God would send to save his people. Often these prophecies had been read in the synagogue on the Sabbath day. The people had almost learned them by heart.

As Jesus stood up to read from the prophecies of Isaiah, the people listened very attentively. He opened the roll to the sixty-first chapter, the first verse. These are the words that he read:

"The Spirit of the Lord is upon me, because he anointed me to preach good tidings to the poor; he hath sent me to proclaim release to the captives, and recovering of sight to the blind; to set at liberty them that are bruised; to proclaim the acceptable year of the Lord."

When he had read this to the people, Jesus rolled up the book and gave it to the attendant. Then he sat down—for it was the custom in those days for the speaker to sit. The people listened closely. They had heard strange reports of his teachings and of his miracles.

"This day, these words that I have read have come true," said Jesus. Of course he meant by this that he was the one whom God had appointed to preach the gospel to the poor, to free the captives, to give sight to the blind, to deliver the prisoners, and to preach the coming of the Lord.

How do you think the people felt as they listened? You would think they would be saying, "The Christ is here at last! What a great honor has come to us, that he should be one of our citizens! How proud we should be that we have known him all his life!"

But Jesus knew that his own people would not believe on him as the people of Jerusalem and Samaria did. They wanted only to see his miracles, but they would not believe that he was the Christ.

"How can this be the Christ?" they wondered. "He is only a carpenter's son. We know his family—his mother Mary, and his brothers. They are common people, just like us. What right has he to claim to be the Christ? Let him perform some miracles for us!"

As they listened, the people became angry and hateful. They rose up and pushed Jesus out of the synagogue, for they would not let him speak any longer.

The city of Nazareth was built on a high hill. Several of its streets ended just at the top of a steep cliff. The furious mob pushed Jesus along one of these streets, intending to shove him over the cliff and kill him.

The evil which the people had in their hearts was not carried out, for they had no power over the Son of God. Jesus passed through the midst of them, and went his way.

CHAPTER 16

The Crowd at Jesus' Door

MATTHEW 8; MARK 1; LUKE 4

After the people of Nazareth tried to kill him, Jesus went to Capernaum. This town was built on the shore of a beautiful lake called the Sea of Galilee.

The people of Nazareth did not see any of Jesus' wonderful miracles because they would not believe on him. He healed only a few sick folk there. The people of Capernaum, however, were eager to have Jesus with them. He taught in their synagogue every Sabbath day, and because they were so anxious to listen to his wonderful words, Jesus spent a great deal of time with them.

The people were astonished at the words which Jesus spoke, for he talked as if he had a right to tell them about God, and to give them commandments. And indeed he had the right to teach about God, for he was the Son of God. When the people heard his words, it seemed to them that a great light had come into their souls.

One day, after teaching in the synagogue, Jesus went to the house of Simon Peter, who lived in Capernaum. In Peter's house there was an old lady who was very sick with a fever. She was Peter's wife's mother. When Jesus learned about her illness, he came to the lady's bedside and took hold of her hands. Lifting her up, he commanded the fever to go away. Immediately the fever left the old lady, and she was able to help prepare the supper.

This same Sabbath day, when the sun was setting, the people of Capernaum brought their sick friends to Jesus. It seemed that the whole city was gathered together at his door. They came at the end of the day, because they did not want to break the Sabbath which lasted till the sun went down. For the Jews, each day begins at sunset, and lasts until the next sunset.

When Jesus saw this great crowd, he laid his hands upon them and healed them. Jesus came into the world to heal people from sin and its results. Sickness was one of the things which sin had brought into the world. Jesus was glad to heal people and to help them.

The day after the Sabbath Jesus got up very early in the morning, long before it was light. He went by himself into a quiet place, where there was no danger that anyone might come and disturb him, for he wanted to talk to his Father in heaven. He often went away alone, so that he could talk to God. Jesus loved God perfectly, and it made him happy to be alone with God and to please Him.

When the morning came, the disciples and the people could not find Jesus. They became worried. Where could their wonderful teacher and healer be? Would they never see him again?

At last they found him in the desert, where he had gone to pray. They gathered close around him, and begged him to stay with them. But Jesus replied, "I must go to the other cities also. God has sent me to teach all the people."

Through all the cities of that part of Galilee Jesus went, preaching in the synagogues and healing the sick. The people who loved him most said to themselves, "Well, if he cannot stay with us, we shall have to go with him. We must be close to him to hear his teaching and to see his miracles."

And so, as Jesus went from one city to another, great crowds of people followed him.

CHAPTER 17

Through the Roof to Jesus

Mark 2; Luke 5

After teaching in many of the towns of Galilee, Jesus went again into the city of Capernaum. As soon as the people of the town saw that their beloved teacher had come back to them, they ran to see him. There was such a crowd that the house could hold no more people, and even outside the door there were throngs.

There were some people in the city who had a poor, sick man in their house. This man could not walk because his whole body trembled and shook. He had to lie in bed all the time, and his family had to feed and dress him.

No doubt this sick man had heard of all the people whom Jesus cured on his first visit to Capernaum. He had not been able to go to Jesus to be cured at that time, because he was not well enough to walk.

As he lay on his bed this man heard a great noise outside. What could it be? Soon three or four of his friends rushed in. "The Master has come again!" they cried. "This time you must go to him and he will make you well. We are going to carry you to him."

Each of the friends took a corner of the mattress on which the sick man lay. They carried him out of the house along the street till they reached the place where Jesus was. But when they reached this house they discovered that they could not get in. They could not even come near the door, because of the great crowd that had come to see Jesus. It seemed that all the sick and lame and blind of the whole city were gathered before the door.

What a disappointment for the poor man and his friends! But having come this far, they were determined to reach Jesus somehow. At last they thought of a plan.

Outside the house there was a stairway leading to the roof. In that country such stairways are very common. The houses are only one story high, and the people often spend much time on the flat roofs of their homes. Sometimes they sleep there on hot nights.

Up this outside stairway the friends of the sick man carefully bore him, until they were upon the roof. They laid him down and began to pull up the tiles of which the roof was made. When they had made a large hole, they tied a strong rope to each corner of the mattress. Then, with one man at each corner, very carefully they lowered the bed right down into the room in front of Jesus.

Jesus was glad to see that these people were eager to get their friend cured, and that they truly believed that Jesus could heal him. But the Master did not say to the sick man, "I will heal you." He said something more startling: "Son, I have forgiven your sins."

Among the great crowd of people round about, there were many wise scribes and Pharisees who had come to see Jesus and to listen to him. When they heard Jesus say, "I have forgiven your sins," they began to say to themselves, "What right has any man to say such things as this? No one can forgive sins except God."

Of course it is quite true that only God can forgive sins. What the Pharisees would not believe was that *Jesus is God.* He said to the man, "I have forgiven your sins," just in order to make them understand that he was God.

Jesus could read the thoughts of the Pharisees and scribes. Knowing that they were finding fault with his words, Jesus said, "Why do you think that I have no right to forgive sins? I will prove to you that I am God, and that I have a right to forgive sins. I shall do something that only God can do." Turning to the sick man, he said, "Rise up, and take your bed, and walk to your house."

The sick man, who for a long time had been unable to walk, rose up like a well man, rolled his rug under his arm, and walked away.

No doctor could have cured a man in this way. It showed that Jesus was not man, but God; and being God, he could also forgive sins. And just as he forgave this man's sins, so if we today pray to him in Heaven, he will forgive us our sins.

CHAPTER 18

Matthew and His Feast

MATTHEW 9; MARK 2; LUKE 5

Every day a man named Matthew sat by the side of one of the main roads near Capernaum. He collected taxes from the Jews for the Roman government, and the main road leading through the city was a place where the people could conveniently come to pay the money.

One day Jesus happened to walk along this road with his friends. He said to Matthew, "Follow me," for he wanted the tax-gatherer to be with him all the time as one of his disciples. Matthew was glad to be chosen. He rose and followed Jesus at once.

From that time on Matthew was one of Jesus' fast friends, who followed him wherever he went. Many years later he wrote the first book of the New Testament, telling about the life of Jesus.

The first thing that Matthew did after Jesus called him to be a disciple was to invite Jesus and the rest of the disciples to a fine party in honor of his new Master. Most of Matthew's guests were tax-gatherers or publicans such as Matthew had been before Jesus called him.

No people were more scorned than these publicans, because they worked for the Roman government. The Jews hated the Romans. They wanted a king of their own. They hated to pay taxes to the Romans, and they despised the people who collected the taxes. Besides, many of the publicans were dishonest and made the Jews pay more than was right.

Most of the Jews would have nothing to do with the tax-gatherers, but the Pharisees hated them most of all. These Pharisees thought themselves much better than any other men, and they would never dream of talking with publicans. They were surprised to see Jesus eating with Matthew and his friends. "Why does your teacher eat with publicans and sinners?" they asked the disciples.

Jesus heard the question, and he did not wait for his disciples to answer. He said, "People that are well do not need a doctor. I did not come to call good people, but to tell sinners to be sorry for their sins."

He meant to say, "I am the great doctor; I have come to cure the worst sickness, which is sin. You Pharisees think that you are good and that you do not need me. These people know that they need me. If they are great sinners, they are just the ones I have come on earth to help. That is why I eat with them."

CHAPTER 19

The Withered Hand Made Well

MATTHEW 12; MARK 3; LUKE 6

One of the laws which the scribes and Pharisees were most strict about keeping was the law of Sabbath rest. We, too, rest from our every-day work on the Lord's Day. But the scribes and Pharisees were so strict that on the Sabbath they would not even help a person who was in trouble or pain.

One Sabbath day Jesus went to the synagogue, as usual. There was a great crowd to hear him teach. Among them were some Pharisees.

As Jesus stood up in the synagogue he could plainly see a man whose right hand was withered and useless. The scribes and Pharisees knew that this man was among them, and they knew that Jesus had healed other men on the Sabbath. They watched to see if Jesus would heal on the Sabbath again.

Jesus knew what they were thinking. After the service was over he called to the man to stand up where every one could see him. Then Jesus said to the Pharisees, "Is it lawful on the Sabbath day to do good or to do harm, to save a life or to destroy it?"

No one answered a word. Jesus turned to the man and said, "Stretch forth your hand." The man lifted his helpless hand, which he had not been able to use for many years. It was perfectly well!

The people adored Jesus because he was always ready to help them also, just as he healed this man. The Pharisees were so busy keeping the rules they had made that they had little time to think of any one else. But when Jesus helped the people and told them about his Father in heaven, many believed him to be the Son of God. Crowds followed him. The scribes and Pharisees became very jealous. They hated Jesus because he did not look up to them and because he often spoke against their teachings.

Seeing him heal this man on the Sabbath day, the Pharisees were mad with anger. They said one to another, "We must do something to stop this man from teaching and doing miracles."

But Jesus went upon the mountain to pray. He was so happy in talking to his Father, that he continued praying all night. When the daylight came he called his disciples upon the mountain. He chose twelve of them to be his special followers, or apostles. After he had gone away from the earth, these men were to tell the whole world what they had seen and heard.

The twelve whom Jesus chose were Peter and his brother Andrew; James and his brother John who were the sons of Zebedee; Philip; Bartholomew, who came to Jesus at the beginning of his teaching; Thomas; and Matthew the publican, who had held a feast for Jesus. Then there was another James and his brother Judas who were the sons of Alpheus; and Simon; and Judas Iscariot.

These twelve men stayed close to Jesus for about two years more, until his work on earth was finished.

CHAPTER 20

The Sermon on the Mount

MATTHEW 5-7; LUKE 6

Seeing the great multitude of people following him, Jesus went up the side of a mountain and sat down where all the people could see and hear him. The disciples sat beside him, with the other people all around. For a long time he talked to them.

Don't you wish that you could have been one of the people who sat on the hillside that day and listened to Jesus? We can not see him and hear him as they did that day. But even though we live many years later, we too may know what Jesus said as he talked to the people.

One of Jesus' disciples was Matthew, who had been a tax-collector when Jesus called him. God told Matthew to write down Jesus' words, so that this wonderful Sermon on the Mount would not be forgotten. God helped him to write it without a mistake. So, you see, Jesus spoke those words not only to the great crowd of people who were sitting on the mountain-side before him, but to us and to all the people in the world.

These are some of the things which Jesus said that day:

"Blessed are they that hunger and thirst after righteousness, for they shall be filled." Jesus meant that those people are blessed whose longing to be good is just as real as hunger and thirst. God gives good hearts to those who long for them.

"Blessed are the merciful, for they shall obtain mercy," Jesus told the people. If we are kind to those who are weak and sinful and suffering, God will remember it, and will be kind to us when we are weak and sinful.

Jesus also said, "Blessed are the pure in heart, for they shall see God. Blessed are the peacemakers, for they shall be called sons of God."

You have the blessing of Jesus when you try to do right, although your companions may make fun of you and try to stop you. When men sneer at you and say bad things about you because you are trying to do the right, do not be discouraged. Be glad, for you will have a great reward in heaven. The prophets of long ago were treated in the same way.

Jesus gave encouragement to his disciples and to all who were trying to please him. "You are the light of the world," he said. "Let your light shine before men, that they may see your good works and glorify your Father who is in heaven." When we love Jesus and try to be good, we are shining for him.

Jesus went on, "You have heard that it was said, 'You ought to love your neighbor and hate your enemy.' But I say unto you, love your enemies, bless those who curse you, and pray for those who persecute you. If you love only those who love you, you do not deserve a reward, for even sinners do the same. But you should be perfect, as your Father in Heaven is perfect.

"If someone does a thing which hurts you, forgive him; for you do many wrong things, and your heavenly Father forgives you. If you do not forgive those who wrong you, neither will your Heavenly Father forgive the bad things which you do.

"Trust God to take care of you, for He knows everything you need. Remember how God takes care of the birds, and of the lilies of the field. They do not work hard, yet God takes care of them. Will He not much more take care of you?"

As Jesus was telling the people these things they listened very quietly, so that they would not miss a word. The things which Jesus spoke seemed very wonderful to them, for he talked as if he knew God, as if he had come down from heaven to bring them a message from their Heavenly Father. Many times he spoke as if he were God himself, and the people were awed.

When Jesus first began to teach, the people thought he was only a wise prophet or teacher, but as they listened to him and saw his miracles, many began to believe that he was truly the Christ, the promised Savior.

CHAPTER 21

Jesus Gives Back Health and Life

MATTHEW 8; MARK 1; LUKE 5, 7.

After talking to the people for a long time on the mountain side, Jesus went down the mountain, with the great crowd of people following him and his disciples. Some of them were sick and lame and blind, and were hoping that Jesus would heal them. All the people, the sick and the well alike, tried to keep far away from one man who had listened to Jesus, and who was now following him.

This man had the terrible disease called leprosy. The dark red patches that had covered his body had already become sores. His hair and nails were falling out and his body was gradually wasting away. No cure for this sickness was known at the time of Jesus. And lepers were not allowed to live with other people or come near them.

Sick and lonely and unhappy, the leper came as near to Jesus as he dared. He kneeled down and bowed his head to the ground, saying, "Lord, if you are willing, you can make me well."

Jesus was not afraid of the dreadful disease. He stretched out his hand and laid it tenderly on the leper's shoulder and said, "I am willing. Be made well." Immediately the man's sores disappeared, and his flesh became clean and fresh and healthy.

Jesus told the man not to tell anyone of his cure, but to go to the priest and make the offering which Moses had commanded. But the man could not be silent. He began to tell everybody he met about the marvelous thing that had happened to him. He told the news of his cure through the whole city.

It was hard for the people to believe that anyone having the dreadful disease of leprosy could be cured. Soon, however, a much more wonderful thing happened, so that they could no longer doubt Jesus' power.

Jesus had gone to a city called Nain. His disciples were with him as usual. Many others who were merely curious about his teaching and his miracles were walking along with them.

As Jesus and his companions came near to the city of Nain, they met a funeral procession. A young man of the city had died, and the people were taking his body to be buried. It was a sad procession, for this young man was his mother's only son, and her husband was dead.

Jesus saw the weeping mother and said to her tenderly, "Do not cry." He motioned with his hand; the men who were carrying the young man's body stood still. "Young man, rise up!" said the Master. And at those words the one who had been dead sat up and began to speak.

Everyone gasped in awe. Since the world began, no doctor has ever been able to bring a dead man back to life. Only God can do that. The people who saw this miracle began to glorify God, saying, "A great prophet has risen up among us!" "God has visited His people!" And the people began to call Jesus "Lord."

CHAPTER 22

Stories Which Jesus Told

MATTHEW 13; MARK 4; LUKE 8

One day, as Jesus went about preaching, he sat down by the shore of the beautiful blue Sea of Galilee. When the people saw Jesus sitting by the seashore, a great multitude gathered together to hear him speak.

While the people stood on the beach Jesus went into a boat, so that they all could see and hear him. As they listened, Jesus told them some stories which had a double meaning. These stories which have a hidden meaning are called parables.

The first story that Jesus told was the Parable of the Sower.

There was a man who went to sow seed in his field. As he sowed, some seeds fell by the wayside, and the birds came and ate them. Others fell in the rocky places where there was not much earth. At once these seeds sprang up, because they had had not much deepness of earth; but when the sun was risen they were scorched and withered away, because they had no root.

Other seeds fell among the thorns, and the thorns grew and choked the good plants. And still other seeds fell upon the good ground, and grew up and bore fruit; some a hundred-fold, some sixty-fold, and some thirty-fold.

After Jesus had told this little story he explained the parable to his disciples, telling them its meaning.

The seed is the word of God. When people hear God's word without understanding it, immediately Satan comes and takes away the words which they have heard, and they forget them. These are the seeds which are sown by the wayside, which the birds eat.

Those that are sown in rocky places are those who hear the word of God with joy, but have no root in themselves. When trouble comes, or when they are laughed at for being Christians, they give up. They believe only for a little while.

Those that are sown among thorns are those who hear the word of God, but are busy with the cares of this world and with trying to get rich. The word they have heard is choked with other things. They do not bring any fruit to perfection.

Those that are sown upon good ground are those who hear God's word and understand it and let it grow in their lives in goodness and love.

Jesus told the people another little story or parable. He said, "The kingdom of heaven is like a man who sowed good seed in his field. In the night-time his enemy came and sowed weeds among the wheat, and went away again.

"Of course, when the wheat grew up the weeds grew up too. The man's servants came to him and said, 'Sir, did you not sow good seed in your field? Then why is it full of weeds?'

"The man said, 'An enemy has done this.'

" 'Shall we go and pull up the weeds?' asked the servants.

"The master said, 'No, there would be too much danger of rooting up the wheat at the same time. Let them both grow together till the harvest time, and then I will give orders to the reapers to gather up the weeds and burn them, and gather the wheat into my barn.' "

Afterwards, when Jesus went into the house where he was staying, the disciples asked him to explain the parable of the wheat and the weeds. He said to them, "I am the one who sows good seed. The field is the world; the good seed are the good people; and the weeds are the wicked people. The enemy that sowed them is the devil; the harvest is the end of the world; and the reapers are the angels.

"As the weeds are gathered up and burned with fire, so shall it be in the end of the world. I will send my angels, and they will gather out of my kingdom all the wicked people and will cast them into the furnace of fire. But the good people shall shine forth as the sun in the kingdom of their Father."

Is it any wonder that those who heard this preaching were surprised? If Jesus were just an ordinary man, as the Pharisees thought, how could he say such things as this: "In the end of the world I will send my angels, and they will gather out of my kingdom all the wicked people, and will cast them into the furnace of fire"?

No wonder the people were surprised. No wonder that they said, "No man ever spoke like this."

CHAPTER 23

The Winds and the Waves Obey

MATTHEW 8; MARK 4; LUKE 8

For several days Jesus continued teaching the people by the Sea of Galilee, telling them parables and healing their sick. After a time he became very tired, for the people were so eager to hear him that they gave him no rest. One day he said to his disciples, "Let us row over to the other side of the lake."

Being very tired, Jesus went into the stern of the boat, where he could lie down and rest upon a soft pillow while the disciples rowed. The rocking motion of the boat was soothing, and the worn-out Jesus soon fell asleep on the cushion.

There is no sweeter place to sleep than on the water, with the oars keeping time, and the boat softly rocking, and the breezes gently blowing. Jesus' disciples, who loved him dearly, were very glad to see their teacher resting.

But soon a change came over the sky. Dark clouds began to form. Puffs of wind began to blow, and the lake no longer was smooth. Big waves began to break against the boat, and the spray dashed over the disciples.

Jesus slept on. The sailors bent to their oars and labored with all their might. The sky grew blacker, the wind howled, and the waves tossed and beat into the boat, so that soon the bottom of the boat was full of water. The disciples were good sailors, but they were terrified now.

If only Jesus were awake, he could help them! At last, in an agony of fear, they woke him. "Teacher! Do you not care that we are going to be drowned?"

Jesus looked out over the raging water and the stormy sky. Then he said quietly to the sea, "Peace, be still."

The wind dropped, the sea grew calm, and the black clouds drifted away. In a few minutes, instead of the roaring storm and the raging billows and the black clouds and the howling wind, there was a blue sky, and a quiet sea, and a soft, still air, as the boat gently slipped over the rippling waves.

The disciples gazed in wonder at the marvellous change that had come over the water. They looked in amazement at Jesus. Who could this be who could make even the wind and the sea obey him? They began to be frightened at the knowledge that it was the Son of God who was with them in the boat. They knew that only God could rule the wind and waves, and raise the dead.

When the boat reached the other side of the Sea of Galilee, Jesus stayed there for a while teaching and healing. After a few days he went back again to Galilee, across the lake. A great crowd of people met on the seashore, for they had heard that Jesus was coming back to them. As he stepped out of the boat they gathered around him to welcome back the great teacher whom they loved. .

CHAPTER 24

The Little Girl Brought to Life

Matthew 9; Mark 5; Luke 8

In the city where Jesus now was, lived a rich man named Jairus. He was a ruler of the synagogue, and therefore a very important man. His only child was a daughter, twelve years old, whom he loved dearly.

One day the little girl became very ill. In spite of everything that was done, she grew worse every hour. Her cheeks were hot with fever. As the agonized father and mother watched her, they realized that in a very short time their child would die.

While they sat by her bed, they heard someone crying in the street, "The Master has come back!" Then they heard the sound of hurrying feet, as people passed by on their way to the seashore.

The mother said, "Go quickly! Beg him to come! *He* can save her!"

Jairus ran as fast as he could to the seashore. When he saw Jesus, he fell down and begged the Master to come and see his little daughter.

Jesus went with him, all the people following. There was such a crowd that Jesus could hardly walk, for they pressed against him on every side.

In the midst of the crowd there was a poor woman, who had had a bleeding sickness for twelve years. She had been to see many doctors and all her money was gone. The doctors had not been able to help her and she was getting worse all the time.

This poor woman was very timid. She was afraid to ask Jesus to help her, with so many people around. She said to herself, "I will steal quietly behind him, and touch his clothes. If I do only that, I shall be made well, and no one will know a thing about it."

Quietly the woman pushed her way through the throng until she came behind Jesus. She timidly put out her hand and touched the hem of his garment. Immediately she felt in herself that the blood had stopped flowing, and that she was well.

But Jesus turned around and asked aloud, "Who touched me?"

All the people around him said, "Not I!"

Then Peter said, "Master, there is such a crowd that everyone is touching you. They press against you on all sides, and how can you say, 'Who touched me?'"

But Jesus looked around and said, "I know someone touched me, for I felt the power go forth from me."

When the woman heard these words, she realized that Jesus knew she had been cured. She was frightened, but she came before him and fell down upon her knees. The poor woman trembled all over as she made her confession. Jesus was kind to her, as he was to all those who needed kindness. "Daughter," he said gently, "because you have believed in me, you are made well. Go in peace."

How happy the woman must have been, to be spoken to with such tenderness! She surely remembered to the end of her life that Jesus called her "Daughter!"

While Jesus had been speaking to this woman, there was bitter sadness in the home of Jairus. The little girl had died. Someone brought the news to Jairus, saying, "Why should you trouble the Master? It is too late!"

These people thought that Jesus was a wonderful doctor, who could cure all kinds of diseases. They had seen him give sight to the blind, and hearing to the deaf. But that anyone might bring the dead to life seemed so unbelievable that they did not even dream of asking Jesus to do it.

Before Jairus could feel grief at this terrible news, Jesus said quietly, "Do not be afraid, only believe, and she shall be made well again." And so the company went on till they came to the home of Jairus.

The house was full of people, for the neighbors had come to sympathize with the poor mother. There was a great deal of loud crying and mourning. Flute-players were playing sad tunes on their flutes. All this was customary among the Jews when someone died.

Jesus said to the mourners, "Why do you make such a tumult? The child is not dead. She is only sleeping." By that he meant that he would awaken her out of death, as out of sleep.

The mourners looked at him with scorn. Had they not seen the dead child? They did not believe that Jesus' power could awaken the little girl from the sleep of death.

First of all, Jesus made these people go out of the house. The father and mother stayed with their dead child, and Peter and James and John went with their Teacher, Jesus, to the place where the little girl was lying. The fever was gone out of her cheeks now, and she was as cold and still and pale as marble. Her eyes were shut, and her hands were folded over her breast.

Jesus took one of the cold little hands in his, and said to her, "Little girl, rise up." At those words the child's spirit came back into her body. She opened her eyes and looked at Jesus and at her father and mother. Then she got up and walked.

For several days before she died, the little girl had been too sick to eat anything. Jesus knew that she must be hungry, and he said to the rejoicing father and mother, "Give her something to eat."

It was a happy family that night, as the father and mother sat with their dear little daughter and talked about the wonderful Teacher who had done this marvelous thing for them.

CHAPTER 25

The Wish of a Young Girl

MATTHEW 14; MARK 6; LUKE 9

Jesus called his twelve disciples to him and sent them out, two by two, to prepare the way before him. He told them to go to all the cities of the Jews, telling the people to repent of their sins and to be sorry for their wickedness, for the Kingdom of Heaven was soon coming.

The disciples were to go without taking food or money, or even an extra pair of shoes and a coat. In every city the disciples were to find some good people, and to stay with them as long as they were in that city. Jesus gave them power to heal all kinds of sickness.

Soon in every village the Jews began to hear about these new preachers. The disciples went throughout the land healing the sick, telling the people to repent of their sins, and teaching about their Master.

Finally the fame of Jesus reached the ears of King Herod. The tales about this marvelous teacher worried Herod, because they reminded him of an evil thing which he had done.

The king had good reason to be troubled. Some time before, he had divorced his own wife and had married the wife of his brother Philip. This was a great sin, and John the Baptist had dared to tell Herod that he had done wrong.

Herod knew that he had sinned, but he was extremely angry with John for daring to reprove him. He sent some of his soldiers out to the Jordan River, where John was preaching, to arrest him and throw him in prison. Herod's new wife was even more angry than the king. She set herself against John, determined to kill him in some way.

Herod would not let his wife kill John, for he knew that the prophet was a good and holy man. He knew, too, that all the people believed John to be sent from God. If he were killed by the king, the people might rise up and mob the palace. Herod kept John safe from the queen, and even listened to his preaching.

While John was still in the dismal prison, the king's birthday came around. Herod made a big birthday party, to which he invited all his lords and high captains, as well as the chief men of Galilee. It was a very splendid feast indeed. During the party the pretty daughter of Herod's wife came in and danced. All the guests were delighted. "What a beautiful girl!" they said, "And how gracefully she dances!"

Herod himself was pleased with her dancing, and with the success of the party. With an oath he promised, "Ask anything you want, even to the half of my kingdom, and I will give it to you."

The girl went out and said to her mother, "Mother, the king was pleased with my dancing, and he promised to give me anything that I want. What shall I ask for?"

The wicked queen had been waiting for just such a chance as this. She said, "Ask for the head of John the Baptist."

The girl hurried in to the room where the feast was being held and said to the king, "My wish is that you give me the head of John the Baptist on a platter."

The king was horrified. He had not dreamed that she would ask for such a thing. He had thought that she would ask for a pearl neck-lace, perhaps, or for a jewel. And yet, he had promised that he would give her whatever she should ask, even to the half of his kingdom. He had sworn it with an oath, in the hearing of all his lords.

The Sermon on the Mount. Matthew 5–7

"There is a boy here who has five barley loaves and two fishes."
Matthew 14

Herod was troubled. He did not want to kill John the Baptist, for he knew John was a good man. Still, he was ashamed to break the oath he had made before all his guests.

Finally Herod called one of his soldiers. He told the man to go into the prison, cut off the head of John the Baptist, and bring it to the banquet hall.

Herod's commands were carried out. Soon the soldier came back, carrying John's head on a platter. The young girl, who had enchanted them all with her dancing, marched out of the room with the platter and gave it to her mother.

The disciples of John heard that their teacher was dead. They came to the prison, begging for John's body. Very lovingly they buried it.

After John the Baptist was dead, Herod's conscience troubled him. The reports that he began to hear about Jesus made him uneasy. Who was this man who could raise the dead? Some people were saying, "John the Baptist is risen from the dead." Others said, "Elijah has come again." Still others said, "One of the old prophets is risen."

Herod was perplexed. He said, "John I beheaded; but who is this about whom I hear such things? He must be John the Baptist, risen from the dead!"

CHAPTER 26

Five Loaves of Bread and Five Thousand People

MATTHEW 14; MARK 6; LUKE 9

After a time, the twelve disciples whom Jesus had sent out to preach in the villages returned to him. Each one told what he had done and what he had taught.

The disciples were tired from their journeys, but there were so many people crowding around them that the twelve had no chance even to eat. Seeing that they needed rest, Jesus told them to go with him into a desert place, away from all the people. The disciples followed him into a boat, and rowed to the other side of the lake.

The people, however, saw this. They ran on foot to the same place, as fast as they could. When Jesus and his disciples reached the other side, there was a great crowd of people waiting for them.

Jesus was sorry for the people, because they were like sheep without a shepherd. They wanted to be taught, and there was no one but Jesus to teach them. So he talked to them all the afternoon.

By and by the sun began to sink, and the evening drew on. The people had been listening to Jesus all the afternoon. Now it was supper time, and they had nothing to eat. In their hurry to run after Jesus, they had forgotten to bring food.

Jesus knows all things. He knew that the people who had been listening to him were now tired and hungry. He said to Philip, "Where can we buy bread enough for such a multitude of people?"

Jesus knew how the people would be fed. He wanted Philip to say, "Master, I know that you have power to feed them." But Philip only said, "Two hundred shillings' worth of bread would not be enough to give every one even a small piece."

Two hundred shillings would be about forty dollars of our money. It was probably more money than all the disciples had together. Philip meant, "Even if we had such a big sum of money, it would not be enough to give them a good supper. We could give each one only a tiny piece of bread."

Although the disciples had been so long with Jesus and had seen him do so many wonderful miracles, they still did not believe that he could do all things. They thought that the best plan would be to send the people away, and let them buy their own food in the villages round about.

Andrew, the brother of Peter, made another suggestion. "There is a boy here who has five barley loaves and two fishes," he said. "But what are they among so many people?"

How stupid and unbelieving the disciples were! Not one of them seemed to know that Jesus was able to feed the people.

"Make the people sit down in groups upon the grass," said the Master.

Soon all the people were seated upon the soft green grass, wondering what new thing the Teacher was going to do. Most of them were men, but there were a great many women and children there, too. The members of each family sat together. When the people were all seated it was easy to count them, for they were arranged in groups of fifty or a hundred. There were about five thousand people there, all eagerly watching to see what would happen.

Jesus took the five loaves and the two fishes. Looking up to Heaven, he thanked God for the food. Then he broke the five barley loaves into pieces, gave them to the disciples, and told them to give them to the people. He did the same with the fishes.

The disciples put the pieces into baskets, and passed them to the people so that every one could take just as much as he wanted. No matter how much was taken out of the baskets, there was always plenty left.

The people at the outside of the gathering were probably wondering if there would be any left, when their turn came. There was enough, and more than enough!

Jesus told the disciples to take the baskets and to gather up the pieces that were left over, so that nothing would be wasted. The disciples gathered up twelve baskets of the broken pieces that were left from the five barley loaves and the two fishes. In the end there was more than there had been in the beginning, although the five thousand people had eaten fully.

The people began to talk excitedly among themselves. They said: "This is certainly the prophet who has been promised for so many hundreds of years! We have heard great teachings from him, and seen many miracles! This must be he! He ought to be our king! There are five thousand of us here. Let us all march into Jerusalem and crown him our king!"

The Jewish people had always expected that the promised Messiah would come as a glorious king, who would lead his people to victory over all their enemies. Then the Jews would no longer be ruled by the Romans. They would have a king of their own in Jerusalem where David and Solomon had ruled.

But Jesus did not come to be an earthly king. He came to be king of the hearts of men. All the people who have ever loved and believed in Jesus are the subjects of his kingdom, the Kingdom of Heaven.

When Jesus found that the people were planning to make him an earthly king, he quietly slipped away.

CHAPTER 27

Walking on Top of the Stormy Water

MATTHEW 14; MARK 6; JOHN 6

While the people were busy planning to make Jesus their king, he told his disciples to get into the boat and to row back over the lake to Capernaum. He would come to them there by and by, he said.

Jesus himself slipped away quietly, and went up into a mountain to pray. Soon the darkness fell and began to cover everything. Jesus was talking to his heavenly Father. He did not mind the darkness. But his disciples, who were rowing on the black water, were afraid.

The Sea of Galilee is a big lake, and the disciples had a long stretch of water before them. It was about four or five miles back to Capernaum. If there had been a bright moon shining in the sky, and if the winds had been calm and still, it would have been delightful to row in the cool evening, after the heat of the day.

But soon the wind began to rise, and the waves frothed with white-caps. The disciples had a hard time to make the boat go against the wind and the waves. It kept swerving first to one side, and then to the other, as the big waves dashed against it. If the disciples had not been good sailors, they could not have managed the boat at all in the rough sea.

While the sailors were struggling to keep the boat safe, Jesus was on the mountain, praying all during the night. Just before the morning light began to come, while it was still dark, Jesus went to his disciples.

How could Jesus reach the twelve, when they were out on the lake? They had been rowing for a long time, and were now far from the shore. How could Jesus cross the stormy water? He did what no man can do. He walked on the water.

When the disciples saw a white figure coming toward them out of the darkness, walking on the water, they were terrified. They thought that it was a ghost which they saw, and they screamed with fear.

Of course there are no ghosts. But even the bravest person would be startled to see a figure in the darkness, walking on the water. Jesus did not want his disciples to be frightened. He called out to them, "Be of good cheer, it is I. Do not be afraid."

Peter was filled with the thought of the wonderful power of Jesus. He felt that Jesus ruled all the world, and that he could do all things. He could even make a poor, weak man like Peter able to walk on the water.

So Peter called to Jesus, "Lord, if it is you, tell me to come to you on the water."

Jesus said to Peter, "Come."

Peter got out of the boat. For a few minutes his heart was so filled with the thought of Jesus' almighty power, that he, too, was able to walk on the waves.

But soon Peter looked around at the howling storm, and as the thought of Jesus passed out of his mind, the fear of the storm came in. When Peter stopped thinking about Jesus, he began to sink. In a panic he called out, "Lord, save me!"

Jesus stretched out his hand and took hold of Peter, saying, "Oh, you of little faith, did you not know that I could keep you from sinking?" With Jesus holding his hand, Peter was not afraid. He thought only of Jesus at his side, and he did not notice the waves. So the two walked on the water till they reached the boat.

As soon as Jesus was in the boat the wind stopped. The disciples were so filled with the thought that Jesus was truly the Son of God, that they came and kneeled down before him, saying, "Truly you are the Son of God."

After they had worshipped Jesus, when they looked around, they saw to their surprise that the boat was close to the shore to which they were going, and that they need not row any longer.

CHAPTER 28

Friends and Enemies

MARK 6, 7

Jesus and his disciples were now near the city of Bethsaida. This was a beautiful country, rich and green. Beautiful bushes with sweet-smelling flowers like roses grew right down to the water's edge.

The people of that country saw Jesus and his disciples landing on their shore, and they wondered a little who these strangers were who had come to visit them. Someone who perhaps had seen Jesus before in some other place soon found out that this man was the wonderful teacher and healer of whom everyone had heard.

As soon as the people discovered who their visitor was, they sent messengers into the country round about, to give word to all the sick people that the healer had come into their country.

Oh, what excitement there was! All the people who had sick friends brought them on mattresses and laid them on the ground near Jesus. The sick begged that they might touch even the border of his robe. As many as touched the blessed Jesus were made perfectly well.

This city, where Jesus was healing the sick, was a long way from Jerusalem. At least sixty miles lay between the two places. That long distance did not keep some of the people of Jerusalem from following the Master. His enemies as well as his friends followed him to hear his teaching.

In Jerusalem there were a great many of the proud scribes and Pharisees who would not have anything to do with other people. These men had made up many rules about serving God. They thought that anyone who did not keep all these rules, as well as the laws given by Moses, was a great sinner.

The scribes and Pharisees were too proud to mingle with the common people who followed Jesus and listened so eagerly to his teaching. They looked down on Jesus because he had not gone to their schools, and because he ate and talked with fishermen and poor people.

But the Pharisees heard many things about this new teacher. Every day they met someone who talked about the great crowds that were following Jesus of Nazareth. "There is no doubt about it," they said. "He does wonderful things. We have heard many times that he cures blind people and deaf people, and men who have all kinds of sickness. We have even heard that he has raised people from the dead. The people are leaving us to follow him."

"Well," said others, "we have heard that he does not teach as we do; so his teaching cannot be true. Why, he even heals people on the Sabbath day. We ought to stop his going around and deceiving the people."

And so some of the Pharisees and scribes journeyed the sixty miles from Jerusalem to the place where Jesus was teaching. They came not to learn from him, but to find fault.

One of the things they criticized was that the disciples did not wash their hands before eating. The Pharisees thought that the disciples were wicked because they broke this Jewish rule. Jesus told them that eating with unwashed hands does not make men wicked. It is not what goes into a man, but what comes out of his heart—killing, stealing, and lying—that is sinful. But the Pharisees became angry when Jesus said that there were things more important than keeping rules.

Even some of Jesus' followers began to leave him, because they did not understand some of the things he said. One day he told them, "I am the bread of life: he that cometh to me shall not hunger, and he that believeth on me shall never thirst. For I am come down out of heaven."

But the Jews said, "This is Jesus, the carpenter's son. How can he say that he has come out of heaven?" And many of them followed him no more.

CHAPTER 29

An Answered Prayer

MATTHEW 15; MARK 7

West of the land of the Jews, on the shore of the Great Sea, lay a country which was small but famous. Its ships sailed far and wide over the seas, and its cities Tyre and Sidon were known through the whole world.

The people of this land did not worship the true God. Most of them worshipped idols and knew very little about the God of the Jews. Some of these people travelled to Jerusalem and came home with very strange stories. A prophet named Jesus had begun to travel through the land with a few friends, teaching the people about God and healing all sorts of diseases. Why, some people even said that he could make the blind see, and the deaf hear, and the lame walk! There never had been such a wonderful teacher! Crowds of people were following him wherever he went, hoping that he would heal them.

Now, after he had spent a long time teaching the crowds that followed him, Jesus wanted to have some time alone with his disciples. There were many things he wanted to teach them about God, but the people would not give them any rest. From morning to night they surrounded him.

One day Jesus led the disciples away from the Lake of Galilee to the west, to the land of Tyre and Sidon. In a village there they found a house to stay in. Jesus did not want anyone to know where he was. But even here he could not be hid. Even here people came to him for help in their troubles. Before he had been there long, a woman came to him in tears and fell down at his feet.

This woman was not a Jew, but one of the people of the land. Although she did not believe in the God of the Jews, she had heard of

Jesus and believed that he could help her. She had come to ask him to heal her little daughter. An evil spirit lived in the little girl and tormented her. The mother begged that Jesus would make the spirit go away.

Jesus said not a word to her. It seemed to her that he was not even listening. But she was desperate, and she believed that he could help her if he only would. She cried again, "Have mercy, O Lord!"

The disciples came and said to Jesus, "Send her away. She is calling out and making too much noise."

Jesus pitied the woman. He wanted the disciples to see her faith, and he answered her, "I was sent to the lost children of Israel."

The woman knew that the Jews were proud of being God's chosen people. She was not one of them. But she kept on begging humbly, "Lord, help me."

Jesus answered, "It is not right to take the children's bread and throw it to the dogs."

The woman knew that the Jews called other nations "dogs," and believed that God did not care for them. But she answered, "Yes, Lord. Even the dogs eat of the crumbs which fall from their master's table." All that she wanted was that her daughter be made well, which would be a small thing for him to do.

"You have great faith in me," said Jesus. "What you have asked will be given to you, because you have believed. The evil spirit has left your daughter."

Joyfully the woman hurried home. The little girl was lying upon a bed, perfectly well. The mother's prayer had been answered.

CHAPTER 30

Hungry People Fed

MATTHEW 15; MARK 8

Day by day, more people came to see Jesus, bringing with them many who were sick. Some were lame, limping painfully along on crutches, hardly able to walk. Others, who had never walked in all their lives, had to be carried by their friends.

There were blind people who had to be led along by the hand. There were deaf people who had never heard a sound, and dumb people who had never been able to speak. There were suffering people with all kinds of diseases.

One by one, Jesus healed the sick. He made the blind able to see, and the lame to walk, and the deaf to hear. Those who had been injured were now well again. Crowds of people watched with joy as they saw their sick friends made well. They were glad, and glorified God.

The crowd was so large that it took Jesus three days to heal the sick. Of course you will ask, "What did all those people do at night?" Galilee is a very warm country. At night the people just lay down on the warm earth to sleep, hoping that the next day their turn would come to see Jesus and be cured.

After the first day, the people had nothing to eat. Perhaps some of them had brought food with them in the first place. That food was soon gone, and the people became very hungry by the third day.

But suppose that you were blind, and had never seen the light of day in all your life. Suppose that you had come to Jesus to be healed, and that you had not yet had your turn. Do you think that you would go home to get something to eat, and lose the chance of having Jesus cure your blindness? No, you would stay close to Jesus, just as those people did, even if you were faint with hunger.

But Jesus knew how hungry those poor people were. When he had cured all the sick, he said to his disciples, "I am sorry for all these people, for they have been with me three days without a thing to eat. If I send them away now, they will faint on the way, for they are weak from want of food. Many of them have a long way to go."

The disciples said, "But where could we get food for them in this wilderness?"

Jesus asked, "How many loaves of bread have you?"

"Seven," was the answer.

Jesus took the seven loaves, and lifting his eyes to heaven, he thanked God for food, as we also ought to do before eating. Then he broke the seven loaves into pieces, and gave them to the disciples to give to the people. There were also a few small fishes, which Jesus blessed and gave to the disciples for the crowd.

The hungry people took all the bread and fish they wanted, and ate till their hunger was satisfied. Oh, how good that food tasted! After the people had eaten, the disciples gathered up seven baskets of broken pieces which were left over.

Some of these people were seeing their friends for the first time in their lives, and their faces shone with happiness that they were no longer blind.

There were people walking who for years had been helpless cripples. There were deaf people, who were listening to the voices of their friends for the first time. There were many who had come in pain and suffering, whose happy faces showed that their pain was gone.

The hearts of the people were filled with love for the dear Jesus who had healed them!

Was there ever such a happy picnic as that one held on the grass among the sweet-smelling flowers of Galilee?

CHAPTER 31

"Who Am I?"

MATTHEW 16; MARK 8; LUKE 9

After a time Jesus again left the Sea of Galilee. He took his disciples for a long journey. They went straight north along the Jordan River, for about thirty miles, till they came to the country of Caesarea Philippi. This was a place where they had never gone before.

As they walked, Jesus asked his disciples a question. 'Who do the people say that I am?"

The disciples answered, "Some say that you are John the Baptist, some say that you are the prophet Elijah, and some say that you are the prophet Jeremiah or another prophet."

Then came a very important question. Jesus asked, "Who do *you* think I am?"

Peter answered, "You are the Christ, the Son of the living God."

Jesus replied, "Blessed are you, Peter, for it is my Father in heaven who has given you this faith."

Jesus was happy to know that his disciples believed that he was the Son of God, the Christ, the promised Savior. They had seen him raise the dead, and walk on the water, and rule the storm. They had listened to his wonderful teaching, and now they knew that he was the Son of God.

Jesus began to explain to the disciples that very soon he must go to Jerusalem. The elders and chief priests of the people would treat him shamefully, and in the end they would kill him; but after he was dead, he would rise again the third day.

Peter was shocked to hear his beloved Master say that he was going to suffer and die. Peter could not believe it. It could not be possible that the Jews would kill the blessed Son of God! Even though the Pharisees hated him, they would never dare do that! Peter said, "Oh, no, that must never happen!"

Jesus turned and said, "Peter, you want to persuade me not to do what I came into the world to do. You act like Satan, when you do that, for Satan would like to have me give up the work which I came to do."

What was this work? Why did Jesus come from Heaven to be born as a little baby?

Jesus came to bear the punishment for our sins, so that we would not have to be punished for our sins. He came in order to die for us.

Jesus knew that the time was drawing near when he would have to go through the suffering of death. He wanted to explain it to his disciples, so that they would understand when it happened. He wanted Peter to know that he had come into the world just in order to die.

Jesus laid down this rule to the disciples: Whoever is willing to forget himself for the sake of Jesus, and to live for him, shall have life eternal. Those who want to follow Jesus and be his friends must not always think about what they want, but must try to be unselfish and to please Jesus.

CHAPTER 32

Glory on the Mountain

MATTHEW 17; MARK 9; LUKE 9

Three of Jesus' disciples seemed to be nearer to him than the others.

Peter was one of these three. It was he, you remember, whose faith was so brave that he tried to walk on the water to go to Jesus. It was Peter who answered, "Thou art the Christ, the Son of the living God."

John, too, was very close to Jesus. He seemed to love and understand Jesus better than any of the other disciples. The Bible calls him, "the beloved disciple." John wrote a part of the Bible, called "the Gospel according to John." This book is so full of love to Jesus that many people like it better than any other part of the Bible.

James was John's brother. He was the third of the disciples who were closest to Jesus.

You remember that it was these three whom Jesus took with him when he raised the little daughter of Jairus from the dead. There were many other times when Jesus kept these three beside him.

One day Jesus took Peter, James and John with him upon a very high mountain. They were going to see something very strange and holy.

While they were upon the mountain, a change came over Jesus. His face shone like the sun, and his clothes became dazzlingly white, like new-fallen snow. On his face there was a heavenly majesty. Moses and Elijah came down from Heaven to talk with him.

While Peter and James and John looked on in awe, a bright cloud came and covered the heavenly group. Out of the cloud came the voice of God saying, "This is My beloved Son, in whom I am well pleased."

If Peter and James and John had had any doubt whether Jesus were really the Son of God, they could doubt no longer. They saw him clothed with heavenly glory. They heard God the Father speak from Heaven, saying, "This is My beloved Son. Hear him." The three disciples fell down and worshipped.

After a time Jesus came and touched the disciples, telling them not to be afraid. And looking up, the disciples saw that the cloud and the figures of the two prophets were gone. Jesus stood there alone. On his face was a look of peace and light.

As they went down the mountain, Jesus told his three followers that he did not want them to tell anybody what they had seen and heard, until after he was risen from the dead. Indeed, the disciples did not want to shout the story out. They felt that they had seen something very sacred. It was too precious to be spoken of lightly.

Never could the disciples forget what they had seen! Never again did Jesus seem to them only a man.

They never forgot that glorious figure—his face shining like the sun, and his clothing so dazzlingly white that they could hardly look at him. After this, to them Jesus was the Lord of Glory.

CHAPTER 33

The Good Samaritan

Luke 10

One day a lawyer came to Jesus and asked, "Master, what must I do to have eternal life?"

Jesus replied, "What does the Bible say that you must do?"

The lawyer answered, "The Bible says, 'Thou shalt love the Lord thy God with all thy heart, and with all thy soul, and with all thy strength, and with all thy mind, and thy neighbor as thyself.'"

Jesus had made the man answer his own question. "Do this," he said, "and you shall have eternal life."

"But who is my neighbor?" asked the lawyer.

Then Jesus told a story, to show the lawyer what loving our neighbor means. This is the story which he told:

There was once a man who went down from Jerusalem to Jericho. The road to Jericho was a rough, wild track. Big stones and rugged cliffs jutted out near the road. It was a place where robbers often hid, in order to spring out upon lonely travellers and strip them of all they had.

As this man was travelling along, a band of robbers sprang out upon him. They took his money and tore off his clothes and beat him so badly that he was near death. Then they left him by the roadside, helpless.

A little while later a certain priest happened to come by. He saw the man lying by the road, but he did not try to help him. The priest did not even go to see if he were alive, but crossed over to the other side of the road and went on his way.

Soon a Levite came along. He too saw the wounded man. He even went and looked at him. But he did not take the trouble to put his hand on the man's heart, to see if it were still beating. He just looked down at him out of curiosity. Then, he too, passed by on the other side of the road.

Last of all, a Samaritan came along the road. He was one of the people whom all the Jews scorned. He had suffered all his life from their hatred. If he had been trying to return evil for evil, he would have hurried past the wounded traveller.

Instead, the Samaritan went over to the place where the poor man was lying. He felt of the man's heart to see if it were beating, and he listened to see if he were still breathing.

When he found that the traveller was alive, the Samaritan took wine and washed the wounds which the robbers had made, and anointed them with olive oil. After a while the wounded man opened his eyes. The Samaritan put him on the ass which he himself had been riding, and walked beside him till they got to an inn.

At the inn, the Samaritan put the wounded traveller in bed and watched over him. The next day, when he had to go on, he gave some money to the innkeeper, saying "Take care of him, and if you have to spend more than this, I will repay you when I come this way again."

After telling this story to the lawyer, Jesus asked, "Which one of these three men do you think was a good neighbor to the man who fell among the thieves?"

Of course, the lawyer said, "The man who showed mercy to him."

Then said Jesus, "Go and do likewise."

CHAPTER 34

The Feast of Tabernacles

JOHN 7

For one week in every year, the Jews held a feast in Jerusalem called the Feast of Tabernacles. This was like our Thanksgiving time, a happy season of rejoicing and praising God for His goodness in giving bountiful harvests. It was held in the fall of the year, about six months after the other great feast of the Jews—the Passover.

A great many of the Jews went up to Jerusalem to keep the Feast of Tabernacles. Most of them were hoping to see Jesus there. Some were his fast friends. Some of them he had healed. Some were merely curious to know more about this teacher whose fame had been growing for the past two years. Others had listened to the Pharisees, and said, "He is not a good teacher, for he does not keep the Law of Moses. He deceives the people."

Before long, Jesus himself came to the feast. He went into the beautiful Temple and began to teach. Some of the people, hearing him for the first time, were amazed. "How can this man speak so well?" they asked. "Is he not the son of a carpenter?"

Others said, "Isn't this the man that the Jews are trying to kill? He is speaking boldly, and they do not say anything to him. Don't the rulers know that this is truly the Christ? He must be Christ, because he does so many wonderful miracles."

When the Pharisees and chief priests heard what the people said, they were furious. They sent soldiers and officers to arrest Jesus and bring him to them.

Jesus stood in the Temple and cried to the people, "If any man is thirsty, let him come unto me and drink." This was his way of saying that if any man has a longing to be good, Jesus will give him the Holy Spirit to live in his heart and teach him to be good.

The soldiers of the Pharisees, who had been sent to arrest Jesus, were listening. They were thrilled by what they heard. "What are the Pharisees thinking of, to want to arrest this man?" they said. "Why, he is a good man. It must be that they do not know who he is, or they would not have sent us to arrest him."

The soldiers went back without Jesus. When the Pharisees and high priests asked, "Why did you not bring him to us?" they answered, "There never was a man in all the world who spoke as this man does."

When the day was over, Jesus went outside the city to the beautiful Mount of Olives, where he spent the night. Early in the morning he went back to Jerusalem to the Temple. All the people came again to him, and he sat down and taught them.

He began, "I am the light of the world. Whoever follows me shall not walk in darkness, but shall have the light of life." It is still true that whoever follows Jesus has a life full of light and happiness.

Jesus continued, "If a man keep my word, he shall not see death." The people did not understand that Jesus was speaking not of the death of the body, but of the soul. "Abraham and the prophets died," they said. "Do you think you are greater than Abraham?"

Jesus answered, "Abraham was glad to see my day."

"You are not yet fifty years old," sneered the Jews; "and do you mean to say that you have seen Abraham?"

"Before Abraham lived, I am," replied Jesus. I AM was the name of God. And of course Jesus *was* God before he came to be a man on earth. But the Jews thought that he was only a man pretending to be the Son of God. They were shocked and angry, and threw stones at him.

But Jesus hid himself and went out of the Temple, and so escaped from them.

As Jesus walked along, he came to a man who had been blind all his life. Instead of passing by, Jesus showed the power of God. Making a little clay, he put it on the blind man's eyes, and told him to wash in a pool near Jerusalem.

Without a question, the man went away and did as he was told. When he came back he seemed like a different person. The sadness had vanished from his face, for he could see! He looked so different, that some of his neighbors were not even sure that this was the man they had known all their lives. "Yes," he insisted, "I am the same man. The teacher called Jesus put some clay upon my eyes, and I washed, and I see."

The Jews would not believe this story until they asked his parents about it. The father and mother were afraid to say anything about Jesus. The Jews had said that if any men should believe him to be the Son of God, they should be put out of the synagogue.

Finally the Jews in anger drove away the man who had been healed. Jesus found him a little while later, and then the man forgot his sorrow at the way he had been treated by the Jews. For no one who has Jesus as his friend can be very sad.

CHAPTER 35

Two Sisters Who Loved Jesus

LUKE 10; JOHN 10

Do you know where Jesus stayed at night, and how he got his meals? He had no house of his own, and no money. Foxes have holes in the earth, and the birds of the air have nests, but Jesus had not even a place to lay his head.

Among those who followed Jesus were some women who used to look after him. When he needed a new cloak some friend gave it to him. He ate and slept with some friend or follower, since he had no place of his own.

In the little village of Bethany, close to Jerusalem, there lived a family which Jesus especially loved to visit. The members of the family were two sisters, Mary and Martha, and their brother Lazarus. All three were fast friends of Jesus, and the Master often visited them.

One day Jesus was staying with this family. Martha was working very hard to cook a nice supper for the Master; but Mary sat at his feet, listening to the wonderful words he was saying.

Martha was not pleased that Mary had left all the work for her. She went to Jesus and said, "Lord, do you not care that my sister has let me do all the work alone? Tell her to come and help me."

"Martha, Martha," said Jesus, "you are working hard over things that are not very important. To listen to my words is the most important thing. Mary has chosen that good part, and it shall not be taken away from her."

From the home of Mary and Martha and Lazarus, Jesus went back to Jerusalem to teach the people. As usual, he went to the Temple. He walked back and forth in the beautiful open space called Solomon's porch, saying, "I am the good shepherd: the good shepherd gives his life for the sheep. He to whom the sheep do not belong, when he sees the wolf coming, leaves the sheep, and the wolf snatches them. He runs away because he is hired, and does not care for the sheep. I am the good shepherd; and I lay down my life for the sheep."

Some of the Jews who were always troubling Jesus, and who did not believe that he was the Son of God, came to him. "How long are you going to leave us in doubt?" they asked. "If you are really the Christ, why do you not tell us plainly?"

Jesus answered, "I have told you, but you do not believe me, because you are not my sheep. My sheep hear my voice and I know them, and they follow me. I will give my sheep eternal life."

Jesus meant that the great multitudes who followed him and believed on him were his sheep. This made the rulers angry. They began to throw stones at Jesus again. The Master said to them, "I have done many good works among you. For which of these do you stone me?"

The angry Jews replied, "We do not stone you for doing good works, but because you say that you are God, although you are only a man."

Jesus said to them, "It is not wrong for me to say that I am the Son of God. You ought to believe me, because I do the works of God."

The Jews tried to seize Jesus, but he escaped out of their hands. He did not stay in Jerusalem, because the Jews would not listen to his teaching. Crossing over the Jordan River, Jesus went to the place in the desert where John had been baptizing at the beginning of his preaching. A great many people came to him there. They were not like the rulers of Jerusalem. These people gladly believed on him.

CHAPTER 36

The Friend of Children and His Prayer

MATTHEW 19; MARK 10; LUKE 18; MATTHEW 6

Some of the people who listened eagerly to Jesus, wanted him to put his hands on the heads of their little children to bless them. "That would be beautiful," they thought. "Our children will remember all their lives that the Christ has blessed them." A few mothers brought their little ones to Jesus, so that he might bless them.

The disciples saw the women coming, and they thought that Jesus was too busy to bother with little children. "You shouldn't bring children here," they scolded. "Can't you see that the Master is very busy? He hasn't time to talk to children."

Jesus had seen the mothers with their little ones. He was displeased that the disciples were sending the children away. Jesus called the mothers back and spoke kindly to them. "Suffer the little children to come unto me," he said. "Forbid them not, for to such belongs the kingdom of God."

Then Jesus took the little children up in his arms and laid his hands on their heads and blessed them.

The mothers went home happy. They never allowed their children to forget that day when the dear Savior had put his hands on their heads and blessed them.

One day Jesus was praying, as he often did. When he had finished, one of his disciples said, "Lord, teach us to pray, as John also taught his disciples." So Jesus taught them the beautiful prayer we call the *Lord's Prayer,* which you have heard many times.

> *Our Father who art in heaven, hallowed be Thy name. Thy kingdom come, Thy will be done, as in heaven, so on earth. Give us this day our daily bread, and forgive us our debts, as we also have forgiven our debtors. And lead us not into temptation, but deliver us from the evil one. For Thine is the kingdom, and the power, and the glory, forever. Amen.*

What does this prayer mean?

Our Father means that God, the great Creator and Ruler of the world, loves us as a father loves his children.

Hallowed be Thy name means "May everyone in the whole world worship God."

Thy kingdom come means "May the time come when all the people in the world shall love God."

Thy will be done, as in heaven, so on earth means "May the people on the earth do what God wants them to, just as the angels in Heaven do God's will."

Give us this day our daily bread asks God to take care of us and to give us our daily food.

And forgive us our debts as we also have forgiven our debtors means "May God forgive us our sins as we forgive those who sin against us."

Lead us not into temptation means "Guide us so that we may be kept from doing wrong."

CHAPTER 37

The Lost Sheep and the Son Who Went Away

LUKE 15

One day Jesus was talking to the crowds of people who followed him. Among them were many publicans and sinners.

Publicans, you remember, were tax-gatherers. They were hated by all the people, because they worked for the Romans and because many of them dishonestly made the people pay more taxes than was right.

When these publicans and sinners listened to Jesus, they were sorry for their sins, and wanted to turn away from them. They crowded around Jesus to hear his kind and loving words. Some of them asked him to supper, so that they could speak with him longer. Jesus was glad to talk with them.

Among the crowds that listened to Jesus were also some of the proud scribes and Pharisees. These people were shocked to see Jesus talking to sinful men, and even eating with them. They would never dream of having anything to do with such common people!

Jesus knew what the Pharisees were thinking. He told a little story or parable which showed them what he meant.

"If one of you has a hundred sheep and loses one, does he not leave the ninety and nine in the wilderness and go after the one that was lost until he has found it? When he has found it, he will carry it home on his shoulders, rejoicing. He will call together his neighbors and friends, and will say to them, 'Rejoice with me, for I have found my sheep which was lost.'

"So I say to you, there is more joy in heaven over one sinner who turns back to God, than over ninety and nine good people who have not been in danger of being lost. For your Father in heaven does not want to lose even one of His children."

By this story Jesus meant to teach the proud Pharisees that God did not love them one bit more than publicans and sinners. Jesus came into the world to find lost sheep and bring them home to God. There is great joy in heaven over one sinner who is sorry for his sins, and turns back to God.

Jesus told the people another little story.

There was once a man who had two sons. One day the younger son said, "Father, give me my share of the money that you are going to leave to us some day." So the father gave the boy the money which he had been saving for him.

Not many days after that, the younger son gathered all his things together, and went on a journey to a far country. While he was there he began to spend his money foolishly, in all sorts of wild and wasteful ways. Soon it was all gone.

There came a terrible famine in that country. The people began to suffer from hunger. Only rich people could buy the little food that was left; and the young man's money was all gone, so that he could not buy anything to eat. All his new friends deserted him now that he had no money.

Finally, the young man went to a man of that country and asked for work. He was sent out into the fields to feed pigs. He was so hungry that he would have been glad to eat the husks that the pigs were eating, but no man gave him any.

At last the young man began to think, "In my father's house even the hired servants have more than enough to eat, and here am I, dying of hunger. I will go back to my father, and I will say, 'Father, I know I have sinned, both against God and against you. I am not worthy to be called your son. Make me a hired servant!'"

So the young man started out to go home to his father. While he was still a great way off, the father saw him, and ran to meet him; and when they met, the father hugged his son and kissed him.

The boy said, "Father, I have been a bad son. I have sinned against God and against you, and I am not worthy to be called your son."

But the father said to his servants, "Bring the best robe and put it on him, and put a ring on his hand, and shoes on his feet. Bring the fatted calf, and kill it, and let us eat and be merry. For this my son was dead, and is alive again. He was lost, and is found."

By this story Jesus wanted to show the scribes and Pharisees that publicans and sinners could become God's children, though they were great sinners. God is ready and glad to receive anyone who turns back to Him.

CHAPTER 38

Jesus Wakes Lazarus From Death

JOHN 11

After the Jews of Jerusalem tried to stone Jesus, he went to the other side of the Jordan, about thirty or forty miles from Jerusalem. While he was teaching there, sorrow came into the home of his friends in Bethany. Lazarus, the brother of Mary and Martha, became very ill. His sisters were afraid that he would die, unless Jesus should heal him. Hastily they sent a messenger to the Master, saying, "'Lord, he whom thou lovest is sick."

For two days Jesus stayed in the same place. On the third day he said to the disciples, "Let us go into Judea again."

"But, Master," they replied, "the Jews there want to kill you. Why do you go back?"

Jesus replied, "Our friend Lazarus is asleep, and I go that I may awake him out of sleep."

"That is a good sign, Lord," the disciples said. "If he sleeps, he will get well."

Then Jesus told them plainly, "Lazarus is dead."

Thomas, one of them, said to the others, "Let us go with the Master, so that we may die with him if he is killed." For they loved their dear Lord so much that they wanted to die with him.

The long walk to Bethany took several days. When Jesus and the disciples finally came to Bethany, Lazarus was dead and had been in the grave for four days.

Mary and Martha sat at home, mourning for their dead brother, while their friends tried to comfort them.

Word was brought that Jesus was coming at last. Martha ran to meet him. When she saw him she cried, "Lord, if you had been here, my brother would not have died. I know that even now, whatever you ask of God, God will give to you."

Jesus said to her, "Your brother shall rise again."

"I know that he will rise again in the resurrection, at the last day," Martha said.

Jesus answered, "I am the resurrection and the life. Everyone who believes on me shall never die. Do you believe this?"

"Yes, Lord," said Martha. "I believe that you are the Christ, the Son of God, who has been promised to come into the world."

Martha knew that Jesus could comfort her sister. She ran home. Quietly, so that the people in the house would not hear, she said to Mary, "The Master has come, and is asking for you."

Mary got up quickly to go to Jesus. Her friends thought she was going to the grave to weep. They followed, in order to comfort her.

Jesus was still outside the town, where Martha had met him. Mary dropped down at his feet and sobbed, "Lord, if you had been here my brother would not have died."

Seeing Mary and all her friends weeping, Jesus felt very sad. "Where have you buried him?" he said.

They said, "Lord, come and see."

Jesus wept.

They said, "See how he loved him!" Others asked softly, "Could not this man, who has opened the eyes of the blind, have kept Lazarus from dying?"

The place where Lazarus was buried was a cave, with a big stone rolled against the opening. Jesus said, "Take away the stone."

"Lord, he has been dead four days!" said Martha. "By this time his body will have begun to decay."

Jesus asked, "Did I not tell you that if you would believe, you should see the glory of God?"

When the stone was rolled away, Jesus lifted his eyes to Heaven and said, "Father, I thank Thee that Thou hast heard me. I know that Thou hearest me always, but I said it so that those who are standing here may believe that Thou hast sent me."

Going close to the grave, Jesus called, "Lazarus, come forth!"

At those words, the man who had been dead came out of the grave. His body was still wrapped in the linen cloths in which he had been buried.

"Take off the wrappings so that he can walk," said Jesus. Oh, how eagerly the people tore off the cloths and looked at their friend, alive and well.

Mary and Martha and Lazarus had been Jesus' true friends for a long time. Now their hearts were almost bursting with love and worship. The disciples too were full of wonder. And how did the friends of Lazarus feel? They also believed that Jesus was the Son of God.

But when the priests and Pharisees heard the news they were very jealous. They knew that more people would leave them to follow Jesus.

"What are we thinking of, that we do not stop him?" they said to one another. "He is doing many miracles, and if we do nothing about it, soon all the people will be following him."

"He does not keep the law of Moses," said others. "He leads the people astray from God. He even dares to call himself God."

The high priest, Caiaphas, said, "The best way to keep him from doing these things is to kill him. It is better that one man die than that the whole nation be led astray."

So from that day they planned how they could kill Jesus. They did not dare to arrest him publicly for fear of the people who loved him.

Jesus had gone to a place near the desert on the east side of the Jordan, and the priests looked for him in vain. They announced that if any man knew where he was, he should tell the chief priests and Pharisees, so that they might arrest him.

CHAPTER 39

The Blind Beggar Who Called to Jesus

MARK 10; LUKE 18

While Jesus was teaching near the desert, the time for the Passover came near. This feast was held in the spring of the year, at about the time when we have our Easter.

For the last time Jesus prepared to go to the feast with his disciples. For three years he had been teaching the people in all parts of the land and healing the sick. He knew that his time on earth was nearly finished, and that the Jews would soon kill him in Jerusalem.

As he went down the road with his disciples he seemed anxious to hurry towards Jerusalem. They could not understand why he should walk so eagerly towards the city where the Jews had tried to kill him.

Before they had gone far, Jesus stopped and called them around him. What he told them was so different from what they wanted and expected that they could not understand it.

He said, "You know that in the Bible the prophets long ago wrote that when the Christ would come, he would be mocked and killed. All the things that were written in the Bible are going to come true when we reach Jerusalem. The high priests and the scribes will arrest him and give him to the Roman soldiers. They will mock him, and spit upon him, and beat him. In the end they will kill him. On the third day he shall rise again from the dead."

The disciples had always hoped that Jesus would be a king in Jerusalem, as David had been. Even when he plainly told them that he must suffer and die, they did not want to believe him.

"The Lord has need of him." Matthew 21

Roman soldiers in the garden of Gethsemane. Matthew 26

On the road to Jerusalem were many people going to the feast. Some of them joined Jesus and his disciples. He taught them and healed the sick among them.

And as they walked, they came to Jericho. Near the gate of this city a poor blind man named Bartimeus sat by the wayside, begging. When Bartimeus heard the sound of the crowd passing by, he wondered what was the matter. He asked some one who stood near, "What is happening? Why are so many people coming this way?"

"Jesus of Nazareth is passing by," the man answered.

Poor Bartimeus trembled with hope and longing. Oh, if Jesus would only come near him and take his blindness away! But would Jesus see him in the crowd? How near was Jesus? Oh, if he could only see how near Jesus was! The Master might pass by without seeing him, and his one chance to be cured would be gone.

These thoughts flashed through the mind of the blind man. Then he called, just as loudly as he could, so that Jesus could hear him even if he were not near: "Jesus, thou son of David, have mercy on me! Jesus! Have mercy on me!"

He made such a noise, that some of the people were annoyed. They told him to keep still. But the blind man raised his voice to shout, "Thou son of David, have mercy on me!"

Jesus heard the cry. He stopped and told the people to bring the blind man to him. Some one came to Bartimeus and said, "Be of good cheer. He has heard you, and he tells you to come to him."

Bartimeus sprang up quickly. In his eagerness he threw his coat on the ground and forgot all about it. Some kind person took his arm and led him to Jesus. The Master said, "What is it that you would like me to do?"

"Lord, I would like to be able to see," said the blind man humbly.

Jesus knew that Bartimeus truly believed on him. "Because of your faith in me," he said, "you shall receive your sight."

At once poor Bartimeus, who never in all his life had been able to see, had the use of his eyes. With great joy he joined the crowd of people following Jesus, and went with them to Jerusalem.

CHAPTER 40

Mary's Gift

MATTHEW 26; MARK 14; JOHN 12

As Jesus and his followers travelled to Jerusalem, he taught them many things. At last they reached the Mount of Olives, which was opposite Jerusalem. Here was the little town of Bethany, and the home of Lazarus, whom Jesus had raised from the dead. There was no one in Bethany so eager to see Jesus as Mary and Martha and their brother.

In that town there lived a man named Simon. He had once been a leper, but Jesus had cured him. This man too was glad to see Jesus again. He made a fine supper for the Master, and invited his friends and all the disciples. Lazarus was one of the guests, while Martha helped to serve the dinner.

In those days people did not sit in chairs before the table when they ate. The table was shaped like a letter "U". The guests lay on couches, with their heads towards the table and their feet away from it.

During the meal, Mary, the sister of Lazarus, came into the supper room carrying a white alabaster box. Inside the box was a very costly and sweet-smelling ointment called spikenard. This perfume was so precious that after it was put into the box the lid was sealed shut. The only way to get the perfume out, was to break the box. Since it was very expensive, it was used only by rich people, or on important occasions.

Mary was not rich, but she loved Jesus very dearly. She was so grateful to him for raising her brother from the dead that she wanted to give him the very nicest thing that she could think of.

As Jesus was eating, Mary came behind him. She broke the box, letting the fragrant perfume fall on his head. Some of it she put on his feet, and wiped them with her hair. The whole house was filled with the sweet smell.

The people who were eating supper looked on in surprise. One of the disciples, Judas Iscariot, was angry. "Why was this costly ointment wasted?" he said. "Why wasn't it sold for fifty dollars and given to the poor?"

Judas pretended that he cared for the poor, but that was not the true reason for his anger. He had been chosen to take care of the money which was given to Jesus and the disciples, and he stole some of it. He had been a disciple for a long time and had seen the love and the power of Jesus, but he did not love the Master.

Jesus knew these things, and he also knew the love in Mary's heart which had made her want to please him. He answered Judas, "She has done a good thing. You always have poor people among you. You can help them whenever you wish. You will not always have me with you, for I shall soon leave you. I am going to die and be buried. By anointing me, Mary has prepared my body for burial. Whoever shall preach about me in the whole world shall also tell what Mary has done, as a remembrance of her."

After the dinner Jesus went to visit Mary and Martha and Lazarus. Hearing that he was in Bethany, many Jews came from Jerusalem, which was only a mile and a half away. They were eager to see Lazarus, too, just as we would want to talk to any man in our town who had been buried and brought to life again.

Many of these people went away believing that Jesus was truly the Son of God. Even some of the chief rulers believed, but they were afraid to say so openly. The Pharisees had announced that if any man should say that Jesus was the Christ, he would be put out of the church. And seeing that many believed because of Lazarus, whom Jesus had raised from the dead, they planned to kill Lazarus too.

CHAPTER 41

The King Comes

MATTHEW 21; MARK 11; LUKE 19; JOHN 12

Many people had heard that Jesus was in Bethany, on his way to the feast. They went out from Jerusalem to meet him, a whole crowd of men and women and little children, eager to see the great teacher.

Jesus sent two of his disciples into the village nearby. He told them, "Go into the village, and you will see a young colt, tied, that no man has ever sat on. Unfasten him and bring him to me. And if any man asks you why you are taking the colt, tell him, 'The Lord has need of him,' and at once he will send him to me."

The disciples went into the village and they saw a young colt tied at the door of a house. As they were unfastening the colt, two or three people standing around said, "Why are you doing that?"

"The Lord needs him," answered the disciples.

"Oh, then you may have him," said the men.

And so the words of a prophet five hundred years earlier were fulfilled. You can read the prophecy in the book of Zechariah, the ninth chapter, the ninth verse: "Rejoice greatly, O daughter of Zion; shout, O daughter of Jerusalem: behold, thy king cometh unto thee: he is just, and having salvation; lowly, and riding upon an ass, even upon a colt, the foal of an ass."

When the disciples returned from their errand, they put some of their clothes upon the colt's back for a saddle for Jesus to ride upon. They were excited and happy because Jesus was riding into Jerusalem, as the kings of Israel had always done when they came to the throne.

The great crowd of people who had come to meet Jesus were wild with joy. They wanted Jesus to be their king. They pulled off their coats and flung them down on the ground to make a carpet for Jesus to ride over. Others cut down branches of palm trees and put them in the way.

All the people shouted with joy: "Hosanna! Blessed is he that cometh in the name of the Lord! Blessed is the kingdom that cometh, the kingdom of our father David! Hosanna in the highest!"

When the parade reached Jerusalem, all the people came out of their houses and gazed in wonder at the crowd waving palm branches and shouting joyfully, "Hosanna! Hosanna to the son of David!"

"Who is this?" asked some. "Why do you shout?"

The multitude answered, "This is Jesus, the prophet from Nazareth of Galilee."

The Pharisees saw the palm branches waving before Jesus as he rode into the city like a king, over a road covered with the clothes of the joyful mob. They, too, heard the people shouting, "Hosanna in the highest! Hosanna to the Son of David that cometh in the name of the Lord!"

To one another they said, "Do you see how little good it does for us to try to stop him? Look, all the people are following him." And some of them said to Jesus, "Master, make your disciples stop all this shouting."

But Jesus replied, "If the people should stop, the very stones would cry out in praise."

And so the Pharisees watched the parade move on to the Temple, while the people went on praising and glorifying God because the Christ had come at last.

CHAPTER 42

The Roman Penny

Matthew 22, 26; Mark 12; Luke 20

Jesus had come near the end of his life upon earth. He had only a few more days to spend with his friends. Every day he taught in the Temple and healed the sick. And everyone was astonished at his teaching. More than ever the Pharisees wanted to put him to death.

Although Jesus taught openly in the Temple, none of the Pharisees dared to harm him. There were several reasons why they did not arrest him.

At this time, the Jews did not have a king of their own, for they were not free. Almost all the world had been conquered by the Romans and had to pay taxes to Rome. Much as the Jews hated it, they were ruled not by a king of their own, but by a Roman governor, whose name was Pilate.

The Romans allowed the Jews to rule themselves in small matters, with the chief priest as judge. But if a man committed a crime that had to be punished with death, he had to be brought to Pilate, the Roman governor. The high priest was not able to condemn anyone to death.

And so even though the Pharisees and priests wanted to kill Jesus because he healed people on the Sabbath and because he called himself the Son of God, they did not dare to harm him. They knew that the Roman governor would not condemn him to death. Pilate did not care whether Jesus kept the Jewish Sabbath, and he did not care if Jesus called himself God. If the Pharisees should bring Jesus before the Roman governor, Pilate would say, "You cannot put a man to death for little things like these."

And so the Jews tried to trick Jesus. They sent men to try to make him say something against the law, so that they could tell Pilate he had broken the law.

One of them asked him if it was lawful to pay taxes to the Roman Emperor, Caesar. Now the Jews hated the Romans, and they hated to pay taxes to Rome. The Pharisees thought that in order to keep the people on his side, Jesus would say, "No, you must give your money to God." If he should say that, they would tell Pilate that Jesus had told the people not to pay taxes to Caesar, and then Pilate would arrest him.

But Jesus knew that they were trying to trick him. He said, "You are only pretending that you want to know. Show me a penny."

They brought him a Roman penny. On it was the picture of the head of Caesar. Jesus asked, "Whose head is this?"

They replied, "Caesar's."

Then said Jesus, "Give to Caesar the things that are Caesar's, and give to God the things that belong to God."

No one could find fault with this answer. Even the Pharisees felt that no man had ever spoken as Jesus spoke. They were overcome by his heavenly dignity, and did not dare to arrest him.

There was another reason why the priests and Pharisees let Jesus alone. They were afraid of the crowds of people who came every day to listen to him as he taught in the Temple. These people loved and believed in Jesus. Do you think that they would have let Roman soldiers arrest their dear Master? Indeed, no! They would have fought the soldiers, and there would have been a terrible uproar.

And so the chief priests and the scribes and the elders of the people met in the palace of the high priest Caiaphas. Again they tried to think of some way to take Jesus by surprise.

CHAPTER 43

The Last Day and the Great Sin

MATTHEW 24, 25

One day, instead of teaching in the Temple, Jesus took his disciples out of Jerusalem, across the brook, and over to the Mount of Olives.

He would be with them only a few days more, and there were some important things he had to say to them before leaving them.

On the quiet mountain side they sat down together. One of the disciples said, "Tell us, how shall we know when you are coming again, and when shall the end of the world be?"

And so Jesus told about his second coming.. When he comes again upon the earth, he will not be born in a stable. He will come as a king upon the clouds of heaven with his angels. Everyone in the whole world will see his return, for he will come as the lightning that shines from one end of heaven to the other. No one knows when that day will come, not even the angels. Only the Heavenly Father knows.

All the nations will be gathered before him on his throne of glory. Those who love him will be at his right hand, and the others at his left.

'And then," said Jesus, "the King shall say unto those on his right hand, 'Come, you blessed of my Father, take the kingdom prepared for you from the foundation of the world: for I was hungry and you gave me food; I was thirsty, and you gave me drink; I was a stranger, and you took me into your house; I was naked, and you clothed me; I was sick and you visited me; I was in prison and you came unto me.'

'Then the good people shall answer, 'Lord, when did we see you hungry and feed you? Or thirsty and give you drink? When did we see that you were a stranger and take you into our house? Or when did we see you naked and clothe you? Or when did we see you sick or in prison and come to you?'

"And the King shall say, "Truly, because you have done it to one of these who love me, even the smallest, it is as if you did it to me.'

"Then he shall say to those on his left hand, 'Depart from me, you cursed, into everlasting fire prepared for the devil and his angels: For I was hungry, and you did not give me food; I was thirsty and you gave me no drink; I was a stranger, and you did not take me into your house; naked, and you did not clothe me; sick and in prison, and you did not come to me to help me.'

"And then shall they also answer him and say, 'Lord, when did we see you hungry, or thirsty, or a stranger, or sick, or in prison, and did not come to help you?'

"Then he shall say, 'Because you did not do it to one of the least of my children, you did not do it to me.'

"And these shall go away into everlasting punishment; but the good shall go into life eternal."

While Jesus spoke these words, there was one disciple who was not listening. Into the heart of Judas Iscariot had come evil thoughts. Because his heart was not filled with love for Jesus, Satan found room in it for a very wicked plan. Satan made Judas want to sell Jesus to the priests and Pharisees, who were trying to kill the Master.

Secretly Judas went to the high priests and said, "What will you give me if I bring Jesus to you when he is alone?" The priests promised to give him thirty pieces of silver (about seventeen dollars of our money).

Of course, neither Judas nor Satan could have harmed the Son of God if he had not let them do it. Jesus was truly God, and far more powerful than Judas or Satan.

It was not the jealousy of the priests, nor the greed of Judas, nor even the hate of Satan, which made the holy and sinless Jesus die. He died because that was what he had come into the world to do. He died because he wanted to bear the punishment for our sins—the punishment which God must otherwise have laid upon us. He died because he loved us. And now if we love him and turn to him, he will save us from sin and death.

CHAPTER 44

In the Upper Room

MATTHEW 26; MARK 14; LUKE 22; JOHN 13

All over Jerusalem the people were preparing for the Passover Feast, which was to be held that night.

Fourteen hundred years before, the Jewish people had been slaves in Egypt. When Pharaoh would not let them go free, God had sent ten plagues upon the Egyptians. Last of all, God had sent the Angel of Death into the Egyptian houses, and in every house the first-born lay dead.

The Jews had been commanded to kill a little lamb, and to sprinkle its blood upon the door-posts of their houses. When the Angel of Death saw the blood, he passed over that house.

The Jews still remembered that night. At the yearly Passover Feast, they sprinkled the blood of a little lamb upon their door-posts in remembrance of the night when the lamb died instead of the first-born.

The Passover lamb did more than remind the Jews of that night. It told the people that some day the Christ would come to die for all the people. Jesus is called the true Lamb of God, because he died to save us, just as the Passover Lamb died instead of the first-born.

To celebrate this last Passover feast, Jesus came to Jerusalem. On the day when the feast was to be held, the disciples came to him and said, "Where shall we go to make the Passover supper ready?"

Jesus said to Peter and John, "Go into Jerusalem. A man with a pitcher of water will meet you. Follow him to the house where he is going. Say to the owner of the house, 'The Master says to you, "Where is the guest room, where I may come to eat the Passover with my disciples?" ' He will show you a large upper room with couches and tables, where we shall celebrate the feast."

Peter and John went into Jerusalem, and found the room as Jesus had said. There they made ready the Passover.

When it was evening, Jesus with his twelve disciples went to that house. In the upper room he sat down with them to eat the Passover. This Thursday night was Jesus' last night on earth. The disciples did not know that, but they knew that he would soon leave them, and they were sad.

As they were eating, Jesus said, "I have wanted very much to eat this supper with you before I suffer." Then he said something that made them forget everything else. "One of you twelve who are eating supper with me will betray me."

They were troubled and grieved. Was one of them going to betray their beloved Lord? One of his own disciples, who loved him so much? How hurt they were! One of them asked sorrowfully, "Is it I, Lord?" Another said, "Is it I?" and the others, "Is it I?"

One of the disciples was lying on the couch next to Jesus, with his head on Jesus' breast. It was John, the beloved disciple.

Peter signed to him to ask Jesus who it should be who would do this wicked thing. John asked, "Who is it, Lord?"

Jesus answered, "It is the one to whom I am going to give this bread, when I have dipped it into the dish."

Taking a little piece of bread, Jesus dipped it into the dish and gave it to Judas Iscariot. As he did so he said, "Woe to that man who betrays me. It would have been better for that man, if he had never been born."

You would think that after hearing Jesus say this, Judas would not do the black deed that he was planning. But Satan came into Judas' wicked heart and whispered that this very night was the time to betray Jesus to the officers. It was night-time, and all the people were in their homes celebrating the Passover supper, leaving Jesus alone with his disciples.

Knowing the thoughts in Judas' heart, Jesus said, "What you are going to do, do quickly." And Judas went out into the night.

None of the other disciples thought that this was strange. They thought that perhaps Jesus had told Judas to go out and give something to the poor, because he carried the purse in which Jesus and the disciples kept their money.

But Jesus knew that Judas was gone to betray him, and that this night would be his last upon earth. He wanted to teach the disciples to remember him. Taking some bread, he blessed it and broke it into little pieces. He gave it to them, saying, "Take this and eat it. This is my body which is broken for you. Do this in remembrance of me."

Then he took a cup of wine and gave thanks and said, "Drink ye all of it. This is my blood which is shed for many."

Since that night, Christian people in all the world celebrate the Lord's Supper by eating bread and drinking wine in memory of the body and blood of our dear Lord, which he gave for us. To those who truly love him and come to him to have their sins forgiven, the bread and the wine of the Lord's Supper are very sacred.

CHAPTER 45

Jesus' Last Words to His Disciples

MATTHEW 26; MARK 14; LUKE 22; JOHN 13-15

After the Passover supper, Jesus said many things to comfort his beloved disciples, before he left them. "Do not let your hearts be troubled," he said. "I am going to my Father. In my Father's house are many beautiful places. I am going to prepare a place for you."

The disciples knew that these were the last words Jesus would teach them. How eagerly they listened!

"If you love me, keep my words," Jesus continued. "My commandment is that you love one another as I have loved you. I am going to lay down my life for you. No man can have greater love for his friends than to die for them.

"When I go to heaven, I will ask my Father to send you a Comforter to stay with you forever. He will send the Holy Spirit down into your hearts to comfort you. When the Holy Spirit comes into your hearts, he will tell you of me."

The disciples remembered these words. And after Jesus went to Heaven, the Holy Spirit came to live in the hearts of those who loved Jesus, to comfort and teach them. For the Holy Spirit is God, just as Jesus and the Father are. These three are one God.

"You have been with me from the beginning, and have heard all my words and seen all my works," said Jesus. "Now I want you to go and tell all the world about me. For I am going to leave you for a little while, and you will be sad. But soon I shall see you again, and then your hearts will be full of joy."

"What does that mean?" wondered the disciples. "Shall we see him again in a little while?" For they did not yet know that Jesus would arise from the dead.

And Jesus raised his eyes to Heaven and prayed. "Father, the time has come for me to leave the earth. I have finished the work which thou gavest me to do. I have given eternal life to those that love thee. I glorified thee on the earth. But now I come to thee. I pray that thou wilt keep my disciples from all evil. And I pray not only for them, but for all the people in the world who will believe on me."

And after this Jesus and the disciples sang a hymn. He led them out of the upper room, and they passed through Jerusalem, over the brook Kidron, to the Mount of Olives, where they had often gone together.

As they walked through the quiet night towards the mountain, Jesus said, "This very night, every one of you will leave me."

The disciples protested. They could not do such a thing! They loved him too much to desert him! Peter cried, "Even if every one else leaves you, yet I will not."

Jesus said to him sorrowfully, "Peter, I tell you truly that this very night, before the cock crows twice, you will say three times that you do not know me."

Peter exclaimed earnestly, "I will *never* desert you. If I should have to die, I would not deny you." And each of the other disciples spoke in the same way. For they did not know what was to happen that very night.

CHAPTER 46

The Kiss of Judas

MATTHEW 26; MARK 14; LUKE 22; JOHN 18

On the Mount of Olives there was a garden called Gethsemane where Jesus and the disciples often went. After the Passover Supper Jesus led the way to this garden and said, "Sit here while I go and pray."

Taking Peter and James and John, Jesus went a little farther into the garden. He said to the three men, "My soul is very sorrowful, even unto death. Stay here and watch with me."

Then Jesus went a little distance away, as far as one can throw a stone. Jesus fell on the ground and prayed to his Father.

Jesus knew that he had come into the world to suffer and die for sin. But when he faced that terrible suffering, he felt as if he could not stand it. He prayed aloud, "O my Father, if it be possible, take away this suffering from me! Nevertheless, not as I will, but as thou wilt!"

In his great agony of suffering, Jesus' sweat was like great drops of blood, falling down to the ground. After a time he rose up from prayer and came to his disciples. He found them sleeping for sorrow.

"Why do you sleep?" he asked. "Rise up and spend your time in prayer. Could you not watch with me one hour?"

A second time Jesus went away and prayed, saying, "O my Father, if I must endure this suffering, thy will be done." And a second time he rose up from prayer and came to his disciples. They were sleeping again, for their eyes were heavy. They did not know what to say; they were ashamed that they could not keep awake when Jesus was suffering.

The Master left them and went away again, and prayed the third time, saying, "O my Father, if I must suffer, Thy will be done." He had wanted his disciples to watch and pray while he was suffering this agony. He was man as well as God, and he needed help in his suffering, just as all men do. Instead of watching and praying, his disciples went to sleep. So God sent an angel down from Heaven to comfort Jesus.

After Jesus had prayed this prayer for the third time, he came back to his disciples and said, "Rise up, let us be going, for the one who is going to betray me is here."

Just then there appeared in the darkness of the garden a sudden flare of torches, lighting up the blackness of the night. In the light of the torches, the disciples could see a band of men and officers, with swords and staves. And leading them was—Judas!

After the supper, Judas had gone to the chief priests and Pharisees and had said, "Now is the time to seize Jesus. He will be alone with his disciples in the garden, where he often goes. Give me some soldiers, and we will soon catch him."

As Judas went along with the soldiers he said, "I will go and kiss him, and you will know by that which one is Jesus." He went forward saying, "Master, Master," as if he were glad to see Jesus, and kissed him.

Jesus knew that it was not friendship that was in Judas' heart. He asked sorrowfully, "Judas, do you betray me with a kiss?" Turning to the officers, Jesus said, "Whom do you want?"

The soldiers answered, "Jesus of Nazareth."

The Master said with simple dignity, "I am he."

The soldiers were awed and afraid. They stepped back and fell to the ground, not daring to touch him.

Jesus said again, "For whom are you looking?" and they said again, "For Jesus of Nazareth."

"I told you that I am he," replied Jesus.

Peter saw that the soldiers had come to arrest Jesus, and he began to think that it was time to do some fighting. He was not going to stand by and let the soldiers take his dear Lord! Drawing his sword, Peter struck off the ear of the high priest's servant.

But Jesus turned to Peter and said, "Put away your sword. Do you not know that if I pray to my Father, He will give me more than twelve legions of angels to take care of me? But how then shall the Scripture be fulfilled?" With these words Jesus touched the man's ear and healed it.

The soldiers closed in around Jesus. Seeing that their master was going to be arrested, the disciples were overcome with terror. They ran away and left him, for fear that they would be arrested too. Peter and John, the beloved disciple, soon came back, to follow at a distance.

CHAPTER 47

Peter, the Coward

MATTHEW 26; MARK 14; LUKE 22; JOHN 18

In the house of Caiaphas, the high priest, all the chief priests and scribes and elders were gathered together to wait for Judas to bring Jesus to them. Towards this house the officers led the way from the garden, with Jesus in their midst. Peter and John followed at a distance, to see what would happen to their Master.

John happened to be acquainted with Caiaphas, and he went into the house when Jesus was led inside. Peter did not dare to go in, since he did not know Caiaphas. He stood outside with the servants.

At last John saw Peter standing there. He told the young girl who waited on the door to bring him in. The girl looked closely at Peter as he entered. "Are you not one of this man's disciples?" she asked.

Peter was desperately afraid that the girl would tell the priests and that he too would be arrested and killed. "No, I am not," he said.

The room in which the disciples were waiting was a large hall, with stairs leading to the place where Jesus had been taken by the officers. The nights are often chilly in that land, and the hall of the high priest was cold. The servants had built a fire to warm themselves while they waited. Peter went and sat by the fire, too.

Standing by the fire was a girl who looked at Peter curiously, and asked, "Aren't you one of his disciples?"

This was the second time someone asked Peter about Jesus. He was more frightened than before. "Truly, I am not," he said earnestly.

But about an hour later, one of the high priest's servants, a relative of the man whose ear Peter had cut off in the garden, asked, "Didn't I see you in the garden with this man? It is plain from the way you talk that you are one of them."

In his terror Peter began to curse and to swear, saying, "I do not know this man."

For the third time Peter denied Jesus. It was now early morning, and just as Peter spoke, the cock crowed. Jesus turned around and looked at him. That look from the Master reminded Peter of what Jesus had said: "Before the cock crows twice, you will deny me three times."

Peter went out of the palace. Oh, to think that he had denied his beloved Lord! And after promising that he would go to prison and to death for him!

Peter's heart was full of grief. He went away by himself in misery. He threw himself down on the ground, and put his head down on his arms.

How could he have done such a thing? He would never forget the look Jesus gave him, when he was saying that he never knew him!

Peter wept bitterly.

CHAPTER 48

Jesus Before the High Priest

MATTHEW 26, 27; MARK 14; LUKE 22

From the garden, Jesus had been led by the soldiers to the house of the high priest. They took him to an upstairs room where the priests and elders were gathered together to question him. It was now late at night, but they were determined to find something to accuse him of before taking him to the Roman governor, Pilate, in the morning. They wanted to make some accusation so serious that Pilate would have to put Jesus to death.

One person after another came and found fault with Jesus, but no two accused him of the same thing. According to Jewish law, at least two witnesses had to agree, before a man could be brought to trial.

No matter what his enemies said, Jesus was silent. At last the high priest rose and asked, "Why do you not answer what these men say against you?"

Still Jesus answered nothing. Then the high priest said solemnly, "I adjure you, by the living God, that you tell us whether you are the Christ, the Son of God."

Jesus replied, "I am, and one day you shall see me sitting at the right hand of God, and coming on the clouds of Heaven."

Triumphantly the high priest said to the others, "We do not need witnesses. Did you hear him say that he is the Son of God? That is blasphemy! You yourselves have heard him. What is your judgment?"

They called out, "He is guilty of death!" They would not believe that he was truly God's son. They thought that he was speaking a terrible blasphemy when he called himself God. According to the law of Moses, any man who thus blasphemed God must be killed.

The high priest, Caiaphas, tore his clothes to show how shocked he was at hearing a man call himself God. The other Jews began to treat Jesus shamefully. They spit in his face. Some of the rough servants blindfolded him and hit him, saying, "Prophesy to us who it was that hit you."

By this time the morning light was showing in the sky. With hate in their hearts, a great crowd of priests and scribes and elders went through the streets of the city to bring Jesus to the house of Pontius Pilate.

In the midst of the crowd that followed was the traitor Judas, who had led the soldiers to Jesus in the garden. When Judas heard the high priest accusing Jesus, and knew that the Master would be killed, he began to realize what a wicked thing he had done.

No one knew better than he that Jesus was the best man that ever lived. Judas' heart cried out, "What have I done! Oh, what have I done!"

Taking the thirty pieces of silver which they had paid him, Judas went to the priests and elders. "Take the money back!" he cried. "I have betrayed innocent blood. Jesus has done no wrong."

But the chief priests replied coldly, "What do we care? That is your own business." They refused to take the money.

Then Judas saw that it was too late. They would not let Jesus go, no matter what Judas might say. He threw the money on the floor, and went out into a field and hanged himself on a tree.

The chief priests picked up the money from the floor. "What shall we do with it?" they wondered. "We cannot give it to the Temple, because it is the price of blood."

Finally they bought with it a piece of land in which strangers might be buried. They called this cemetery "the Potter's Field." Afterwards, the people in Jerusalem heard what had happened. They gave the field another name. They called it "the Field of Blood."

CHAPTER 49

Why Pilate Washed His Hands

MATTHEW 27; MARK 15; LUKE 23; JOHN 18

Early in the morning Pilate saw a crowd of Jewish priests and elders coming towards his palace, bringing with them a prisoner who was bound. He came out and asked, "Why are you bringing this man here? What has he done?"

They answered, "If he were not a criminal, we would not have brought him to you. We found this fellow teaching wrong things, telling the people not to pay taxes to Caesar, and saying that he is Christ, a king."

Pilate went inside the judgment hall and called Jesus to come in to him alone, so that he could examine this prisoner quietly. "Are you the king of the Jews?" he asked.

Jesus replied, "My kingdom is not of this world. If it were an earthly kingdom, then my servants would fight, so that I should not be arrested."

"Are you a king, then?" asked Pilate.

"Yes," said Jesus, "I am a king. I came into this world to tell the truth. Those who love the truth listen to me."

"What is truth?" asked Pilate. He did not wait for an answer, for he did not believe Jesus could teach him. Again he went outside the judgment hall, to the pavement where the crowd of chief priests and elders and other people were standing. "You have brought this man to me to be judged," he said. "I have talked with him, and I can find no fault with him. He has done nothing worthy of death."

But the crowd set up a clamor. "He has been teaching the people to rebel, from Galilee through all the land."

When Pilate heard that Jesus was from Galilee, he decided to send him for trial to Herod, the ruler of Galilee, who was then in Jerusalem. Herod was the king who had put John the Baptist into prison and murdered him. Sometimes when he remembered John, Herod wondered if this new teacher, Jesus, could be John come to life again.

But Jesus refused to answer Herod's questions or to work a miracle for him. Herod sent him back to Pilate, saying that he had found no reason why Jesus should be put to death.

Herod's reply made Pilate all the more sure that it would be very wrong to kill Jesus. The governor's wife also sent a messenger to him, saying, "Do not condemn that good man, for I have suffered many things tonight in a dream, because of him."

Therefore Pilate went out to the Jews and said, "You have a custom that I should release a prisoner every year at the time of the feast. Shall I release the King of the Jews?"

The priests knew that there was in the prison a man named Barabbas—a robber and a murderer. They urged the people to shout, "Not this man, but Barabbas! Barabbas! Not this man, but Barabbas!"

Pilate said, "Then what shall I do with Jesus, who is called Christ?"

The crowd yelled wildly, "Let him be crucified! Let him be crucified! Away with this man! Release Barabbas!"

"Take him yourselves and crucify him," said Pilate. "I find no crime in him."

The Jews said, "We have a law, and by our law he ought to die, because he called himself the Son of God."

At these words Pilate was afraid. What if Jesus were really the Son of God? Pilate went back into the judgment hall, calling Jesus to come to him. He asked, "Where did you come from?" But Jesus answered not a word.

"Do you refuse to answer me?" asked Pilate. "Do you not know that I have power to crucify you, and I have power to let you go?"

Then Jesus said, "You could have no power against me, if God did not give it to you."

Pilate brought Jesus to the pavement outside, where the crowd was, and said, "I find no cause of death in this man. I will therefore whip him and let him go."

Instantly they shouted, "If you let this man go, you are not Caesar's friend. Whoever calls himself a king, speaks against the emperor at Rome."

Pilate saw he could do nothing, but he did not want to bear the blame. He took a basin of water and washed his hands before the crowd, as if he were washing away the guilt. Solemnly he said, "I am not to blame for killing this good man. You are to blame."

"We will bear the blame," shouted the people. "His blood be upon us and upon our children!"

Then Pilate released the murderer Barabbas, and he gave Jesus to be crucified.

CHAPTER 50

Carrying the Cross

MATTHEW 27; MARK 15; LUKE 23; JOHN 19

With joy the enemies of Jesus heard Pilate give the order that Jesus should be crucified. At last he would be put out of the way.

The Roman soldiers bound Jesus to a post. They beat his bare back with a cruel knotted whip, till Jesus' back was covered with blood.

Not content with making Jesus suffer pain, the soldiers began to mock and insult him. Because he had said he was a king, they pretended to treat him like a king. They dressed him in a bright red robe, the color which kings wore.

For a crown, they took some thorny branches and twisted them together into a wreath. This they put on Jesus' head. In his hand they put a reed for his royal scepter.

When the soldiers had dressed him in this way, they began to make fun of him and to mock him. They kneeled down before him, saying, "Hail, King of the Jews." They spit on him, and snatching the reed out of his hand, they hit him with it.

Jesus bore all this without a word. He was suffering these things for us, just as Isaiah had prophesied seven hundred years before Jesus came into the world: *Surely he hath borne our griefs, and carried our sorrows.*

After mocking Jesus, the rough soldiers took the scarlet robe away from him. On his torn and bleeding shoulders they put a heavy wooden cross. Then they led him away to be crucified.

Outside the city wall of Jerusalem was a low hill called Calvary, where people were taken to be crucified. Towards this place the soldiers led Jesus, while a crowd of Jesus' enemies and a few of his friends followed.

It was a long way to Calvary, and the cross was heavy. Jesus was weak and in great pain because he had been beaten. As the procession came out of the city of Jerusalem, Jesus stumbled and fell under the heavy cross.

Just then a strong countryman named Simon happened to be coming into the city. Seeing that Jesus was too weak to carry the cross, the soldiers forced this man to carry the cross for him.

Where were all Jesus' friends? Where was the multitude of Jews who came to listen to him in the Temple, the people who only a week before had shouted, "Blessed is the King that cometh in the name of the Lord"? For many of the Jews did love Jesus.

Most of Jesus' friends did not know what was happening to him, for the priests had been careful to arrest Jesus when no one would know about it. It was evening when Judas came to the Garden of Gethsemane to betray his Master. Jesus had been kept in Caiaphas' house all night, and had been brought to Pilate's judgment hall in the dawn of the morning. Even now it was only nine o'clock. Many people were quietly eating their breakfast in Jerusalem, not knowing what was happening to Jesus. Probably they went to the Temple expecting to hear Jesus teach as he had done on other days.

Soon the news spread like wild fire in every direction. "They have taken our Lord! They have arrested him and are going to kill him at last! Hurry! *Hurry!* They have taken him outside the city to crucify him!"

Many of Jesus' friends came running out of their houses and hastened to the hill of Calvary. The women who had tried to follow Jesus while he was teaching, hurried along the sad road that Jesus had stumbled over a little while earlier. Among them was Mary, Jesus' own mother. Another was Mary Magdalene, whom Jesus had cured.

John, the beloved disciple, had not left Jesus during the long night. He had seen the soldiers beat and mock his Master. He stayed near Jesus all the way to Calvary.

At last the spot was reached. There Jesus' friends could see the soldiers digging the hole for the cross. And as they watched helplessly, grief filled their hearts.

CHAPTER 51

The Sun Becomes Dark

MATTHEW 27; MARK 15; LUKE 23; JOHN 19

On the little hill of Calvary just outside Jerusalem, the soldiers stopped. They fastened to the top of the cross the title which Pilate had written in Greek and Hebrew and Latin: *Jesus of Nazareth, the King of the Jews.*

Then they stretched Jesus out upon the cross. With heavy spikes they nailed his hands and feet to the wooden beams. They raised the cross and set it in the hole which they had dug, and filled the hole with stones and earth, so that the cross would stand upright.

Two thieves were crucified with Jesus, one on his right hand, and one on his left.

When their work was done, the four soldiers took Jesus' clothes and divided them into four piles, one for each of them. The coat that he had worn was without seams, woven from the top in one piece. It would be spoiled if it were cut; so they said, "Let us not tear it, but cast lots."

As Jesus hung from his wounded hands and feet, the blood which was shed for us came dropping down. In his great suffering, Jesus prayed, "Father, forgive them, for they know not what they do."

Around the cross, Jesus' friends had gathered, among them many women. The two whom Jesus loved most of all, his mother and the beloved disciple John, were standing close to the cross. He saw them there, and in his pain he did not forget them. He said to his mother, "John shall be your son," and to John, "Take my mother to be your mother."

While Jesus' friends wept, there were many who rejoiced to see him die. The scribes and priests who had cried, "Crucify him!" had followed to Calvary. Now they jeered and mocked. "Save yourself, and come down from the cross," they called.

"He saved others, but he cannot save himself," others sneered. "If you are Christ, the King of Israel, come down from the cross and we will believe on you."

One of the thieves who hung beside Jesus joined in, saying, "If you are Christ, save yourself and us."

But the other thief said, "How dare you talk like this, when you are so soon going to die and appear before God? You and I deserve to be crucified, because of our wicked deeds; but this man has done nothing wrong." He cried to Jesus. "Lord, remember me when you come into your kingdom."

Jesus answered, "Today you shall be with me in Paradise." And that is the answer which Jesus gives to every dying one who loves him.

At noon God took away the light of day. For three dreadful hours, while Jesus hung in agony on the cross, the darkness of night spread over all the land.

Jesus was suffering from the pain of the nails in his bleeding hands and feet, but now a deeper kind of suffering came upon him. He was suffering because he knew that God had left him.

All his life upon earth, Jesus had loved God and served him. Now he had taken upon himself all the sin that ever has been done or ever will be done in the whole world—yours and mine and everybody's —just as if he himself had done it. And God gave him the punishment that we would have had to suffer, for He left Jesus, and that is the worst punishment that any sinner can suffer.

In his anguish Jesus cried out, "My God, my God, why hast Thou forsaken me?" It is no wonder that in those black hours the light of the sun was withdrawn, and the whole earth was plunged in darkness.

Just before the end, Jesus said, "I thirst." Someone kindly dipped a sponge into a dish of vinegar, and raised it to Jesus' mouth upon a stick.

It was almost over now. Knowing that his work was done, Jesus cried out in a loud voice, "It is finished." Once more he spoke: "Father, into Thy hands I commend my spirit."

Then Jesus' head dropped upon his breast and his spirit passed away. The suffering was over. The work was done. He had borne our sins to save us.

Just as Jesus' soul was passing away, God sent an earthquake. The ground trembled and shook, and the rocks were torn apart. The veil of the Temple, which separated the holiest place from the rest of the Temple, was torn from the top to the bottom. Everyone could look into the Holy of Holies, where no one except the high priest had ever gone before, and he only once a year.

The captain of the Roman soldiers was astonished to see the greatness of the suffering Savior, and the signs of God's anger in the three hours of darkness and the earthquake. "Truly, this was the Son of God," he cried.

And the captain of the Roman soldiers was right.

It was truly the very Son of God who died there on the cross of Calvary. He died there for us. He gave his life to atone for our sins. As the prophet said long, long before, "Surely, he hath borne our griefs and carried our sorrows . . . he was wounded for our transgressions, he was bruised for our iniquities, and by his stripes we are healed" (Isaiah 53).

We may go to this same Jesus today with all our sorrows, all our problems, all our sins. He sees us and hears us and loves us. Believing on Him, we have new life—a joyous, happy life. For he takes away our burdens.

Shall we not love and serve this wonderful Jesus, who finished the work of our salvation upon the cross?

CHAPTER 52

The Stone is Rolled Away

MATTHEW 27, 28; JOHN 19

Among the disciples of Jesus was a rich man named Joseph, who had never dared to serve Jesus openly for fear of the priests. Now that Jesus was dead, Joseph went to Pilate and begged the right to bury Jesus.

Another rich friend of Jesus was Nicodemus, the ruler of the Jews who had once come to Jesus by night. Nicodemus brought a hundred pounds of spices, such as the Jews used to wrap dead bodies in.

In a garden near Jerusalem was a grave that Joseph had intended for himself when he should die. It had been carved out of the solid rock, like many of the Jewish graves. It was here that Jesus' body was laid. A great stone was rolled before the tomb.

It was sunset, the time at which the Jewish Sabbath began. With sad hearts Jesus' friends left the tomb and went home.

The next morning, which was the Sabbath, the chief priests and Pharisees met in Jerusalem. While they were exulting over the death of Jesus, one of them suddenly remembered that Jesus had said, "After three days I will rise again."

None of the priests believed that Jesus really would rise from the dead. But they feared that some of his disciples might come at night and steal his body away, and then tell the people that Jesus had risen.

With this thought, they hurried to Pilate's house and said to him, "Sir, we remember that while that deceiver was yet alive, he said, 'After three days I will rise again.' Therefore we ask you to command that the grave be sealed until the third day, for fear that his disciples might steal him away by night and say to the people that he is risen from the dead."

"You may have soldiers to watch the grave, and you may seal the opening," Pilate replied. "Make it as sure as you can."

So the Pharisees and the priests hurried to the garden where Jesus had been buried. They sealed the stone before the opening, and set some men to watch so that it might not be disturbed.

That Saturday was a sad day for Jesus' disciples and for the women who had followed him from Galilee. They met together in an upper room, where the enemies of Jesus would not see them, and they talked sadly together about what had happened.

These people had loved Jesus dearly. They had never loved any, one so much before. They had hoped that he would set up a kingdom and rule over the Jews, as David had done. But now that Jesus was dead, they were sad and hopeless.

All that day and night, while Jesus' friends mourned together in the upper room, the watchmen stayed at the tomb. Just as the first faint streaks of dawn came into the sky on Sunday morning, all at once the earth began to tremble and shake. In some places great cracks opened in the ground.

The watchmen were terrified, fearing that in another moment the earth would open and swallow them up. While the earth quaked, a mighty angel of the Lord came down from Heaven and rolled away the stone and sat upon it. His face shone like the lightning, and his clothes were as white as new-fallen snow.

In their terror the watchmen fell to the ground like dead men. When they revived, they saw that the grave was open and empty! Then they ran to the city of Jerusalem, to tell the chief priests and Pharisees about the angel and the earthquake and the empty tomb.

When the priests heard that an angel had descended from Heaven to open the grave, they should have believed on Jesus. But no matter how wonderful the signs about him were, they were determined not to believe. They did a most dishonest thing.

They said to the watchmen, "Tell everybody that his disciples came and stole him away while you were sleeping. Say nothing about the angel. If you will do this we will give you a large sum of money. And if Pilate hears about it, we will persuade him not to punish you."

So the Pharisees bribed the soldiers to do a great wrong.

CHAPTER 53

Visitors to the Tomb

MARK 16; JOHN 20

Mary Magdalene and several other women had prepared some spices on Friday night. They had been waiting all Saturday for the Sabbath day to pass, so that they might go to the grave to anoint Jesus' body.

On Sunday morning, before the sun rose, they walked to the garden where Jesus had been buried. "Who shall roll the stone away from the tomb?" they wondered, for they knew it was so large and heavy that they would not be able to move it.

When the women reached the tomb, they found the stone was already rolled away. They stooped and went inside the grave. Jesus' body was not there! The tomb was empty!

The women did not know what to think. As they stood there wondering, two angels in shining white clothes stood by them. In fear the women bowed to the ground.

"Do not be afraid," said the angels. "You are looking for Jesus, who was crucified. He is not here. He is risen! Do you not remember that he said to you that on the third day he would rise again?"

The women remembered that Jesus had said that very thing. They ran all the way back to Jerusalem, to tell the disciples what they had seen. They said excitedly, "We found Jesus' tomb empty! And we saw a vision of angels, who said that he is alive! But we did not see him."

The disciples did not believe the story of the excited women. Had they not seen the dead body of their Lord? They had forgotten that he had told them plainly that he would live again.

It is easy for us today to believe that Jesus became alive again, because for two thousand years people have known that it happened. It was very hard for the disciples to understand it at first. Jesus had brought life to a little girl who had died, but no one had ever raised himself from death.

When Peter and John heard the women's story, they had to go and see for themselves. The garden where Jesus had been buried was more than a mile distant, but in their eagerness to see if he were truly alive again they ran all the way.

John ran faster than Peter, for he was the younger. He reached the tomb first. Stooping down, he saw the linen cloths that had been wrapped around Jesus' body, but Jesus himself was gone.

By that time, Peter had reached the grave. He went past John into the tomb. There were the linen cloths, and the napkin that had been wrapped about Jesus' head lay in a place by itself.

John followed Peter into the tomb. There were no angels to be seen. Even now Peter and John did not realize that Jesus had risen, and that they would see him again. Slowly they went back to the room in Jerusalem where the disciples were gathered.

Mary Magdalene could not stay away from the tomb. She went back and stood there with tears rolling down her cheeks. Indeed, she had done little but weep, these three days. Jesus had been kind to her, and now he was dead. She did not understand that Jesus was alive again, for she had been so greatly frightened to see the angel that she could hardly remember what he had said. Jesus was no longer in the tomb; but where he was, Mary did not know.

After a while she stooped down and looked into the tomb. Two beautiful angels were sitting there, one at the head, and one at the foot of the place where the body of Jesus had lain.

The angels said, "Woman, why do you weep?"

Mary answered, "Because they have taken away my Lord, and

I do not know where they have laid him." As she turned around, Mary saw someone standing before her. It was Jesus. She did not recognize him through her tears, but supposed that he was the gardener.

Jesus said, "Why are you weeping? For whom are you looking?"

Mary still did not know who it was, "Oh, sir," she said, "if you have borne him away, tell me where you have laid him, and I will take him away."

Jesus said, "Mary!" When she heard that beloved voice speak her name, Mary turned and looked straight at Jesus. It was truly her dear Lord! "Master!" she cried.

Mary was wild with happiness. While she looked with love and joy at her dear Lord, he told her to go to his disciples, and to tell them that he was going to ascend to his Father in Heaven.

How happy Mary was as she ran into Jerusalem, to the room where the disciples were mourning! "He is alive!" she called. "He is alive! I have seen him myself! He came and spoke to me in the garden. He told me to come back here and to tell you that he is risen! And he told me to tell you that he is going to ascend up into Heaven!"

The hearts of the disciples had been so burdened with sorrow, that they could hardly realize what Mary was saying. At last they began to believe, and to remember that Jesus had said to them that he would live again, and that they would soon see him. They had not realized that he was stronger than death. Now at last they knew that Jesus is the Lord of life.

CHAPTER 54

The Risen Lord

MARK 16; LUKE 24

On the Sunday on which Jesus rose from the grave, two men were walking from Jerusalem to the little village of Emmaus, not far away. The name of the one man was Cleopas; the name of the other we do not know.

As they walked, they talked about Jesus' death, and the strange story of the women who had gone to the tomb early that morning. In the midst of their talk Jesus himself came and walked with them, though they did not know it was he. He asked, "What are you talking about, that makes you so sad?"

"Are you a stranger in Jerusalem?" asked Cleopas. "Don't you know the things that have happened there in the last three days?"

"What things?" asked Jesus.

They said, "About Jesus of Nazareth. He was a wonderful prophet of God, both in what he taught and in the works he did. But our chief priests and rulers have crucified him. We hoped that he was the Savior of Israel, but today is the third day since these things happened." Both of the men were sad at the thought.

Then they went on. "Some women went to the tomb early this morning. They said that his body was not there, and that they had seen a vision of angels who said that he was alive. Some of us went to the tomb and found that his body was really gone. But they did not find him."

Then Jesus began to speak. "Don't you understand? All these things that have happened to Jesus were written in the Bible long ago. Don't you know that the prophets foretold all these things? It was

Jesus said to her, "Woman, why are you weeping?" Mark 16

Among the first members of Christ's church there was a spirit of love.
Acts 5

God's plan that he would suffer and die for men, and afterwards go up to heaven in glory."

Starting at the beginning of the Bible, Jesus told them all the things in the Old Testament that had been prophesied about himself. He talked until they came to the town of Emmaus, where Cleopas and his friend were going to stay. They begged Jesus to spend the night with them, for it was already evening.

After Cleopas and his friend prepared some food, the three of them sat down to supper. Jesus blessed the bread and gave it to them. All at once their eyes were opened, and they saw that it was Jesus.

While they looked, he vanished out of their sight. For since his death, Jesus could go anywhere without walking there. He could go through closed doors, and into locked rooms.

Cleopas and his friend remembered how Jesus had talked to them as they walked. "Did not our hearts burn within us while he talked with us on the way, and while he explained the prophets to us?" they remembered. Eagerly they hurried back to Jerusalem to tell the disciples the marvelous news that Jesus was truly risen from the dead. It was six miles back to Jerusalem, but they did not care. It was dark, but that made no difference. Cleopas and his friend almost ran in their hurry to tell the disciples the wonderful news.

Jesus' friends were sitting in an upstairs room in Jerusalem. They had shut the doors tight, for they were afraid that the same Jews who had killed Jesus would now try to kill his disciples. They were no longer sad, for Jesus had appeared to Peter as well as to Mary.

Then Cleopas and his friend burst in, with their story of meeting and talking to Jesus. While they were still talking, suddenly Jesus stood in the middle of the room and said, "Peace be unto you."

Instead of being wild with joy, the disciples were terrified. They thought he must be a ghost, because he had come in when the doors were locked. But Jesus said, "Why are you frightened, and why do you think that I am a ghost? Look at my hands and feet, and see that it is I, myself. Touch me, and see that I have real flesh and bones. A spirit does not have a body, as I have."

As they saw his hands and feet, torn by the nails of the cross, the disciples knew that this was their own dear Lord. Their hearts were filled with joy and wonder.

Jesus asked if they had any food in the room. They gave him a piece of a broiled fish, and he ate it to prove to them that he was alive.

Then he asked, "Do you not remember that when I was still with you, I told you that I must suffer and die, as the prophets wrote in the Bible?" He began to explain all the prophecies about himself in the Old Testament, as he had explained them to Cleopas and his friend on the way to Emmaus.

"For this I suffered and died, and rose again on the third day, so that all who are sorry for their sins can be forgiven. Go and preach to all nations, beginning at Jerusalem. You who have been with me and have seen these things are to tell them to all the world. I will send the Holy Spirit upon you. Stay in Jerusalem until the Spirit shall come and give you power."

The disciples listened with joy. How could they be sad and afraid, now that their Lord was living again? Jesus was stronger than death, which had come into the world when Adam sinned. By rising again, Jesus brought eternal life to all who love him.

CHAPTER 55

Jesus Comes to His Friends

Luke 24; John 20, 21

When Jesus appeared in the upper room, one of the disciples was not there. That one was Thomas. When the others told Thomas that they had seen the Lord, he said, "Unless I see the print of the nails, and put my finger into the nail holes, and thrust my hand into the wound in his side, I will not believe."

After eight days, it happened that the disciples were together again in the same room, with the doors shut. This time Thomas was with them. Again Jesus stood in the midst of them and said gently, *"Peace be unto you."*

Turning to Thomas, Jesus said, "Reach out your finger, and put it into the nail holes in my hand. Reach out your hand, and thrust it into my side, and believe."

Thomas could doubt no longer. He said, "My Lord, and my God!"

Jesus said to him, "Thomas, you have believed because you have seen me. Blessed are those who have not seen, and yet have believed."

But though the disciples believed Jesus was living, they did not always recognize him when he came to them, until he let them see who he was. The very next time he appeared to them they did not know him.

It happened this way. The disciples had gone back to the Sea of Galilee, where they had lived before Jesus called them. Simon Peter was a fisherman. With some of the other disciples, he took nets and rowed out into the lake to fish.

All night they fished without success. In the morning, when they came near the shore, Jesus was standing on the beach, although they did not know it was he.

He said to them, "Children, have you anything to eat?"

They answered, "No."

"Cast your net on the right side of the boat, and you will find some fish," he said.

They did as he told them. Now their net was so full of fish that they could not draw it out of the water. Tug as hard as they would, they could not pull it up.

John, who was fishing with Peter, knew that it was a miracle. So many fish where there had been none before! He said to Peter, "It is the Lord."

Peter could not wait to see Jesus. He jumped out of the boat into the shallow water, leaving the other disciples to drag the net to land.

When the disciples reached shore, they saw a fire with fish frying on it, and some bread beside it. Jesus said, "Bring some of the fish that you caught." They brought fish to him. Then Jesus said, "Come and eat." So they ate. None of the disciples dared ask, "Who are you?" for they all knew it was the Lord.

After they had finished eating, Jesus said to Peter, "Peter, do you love me?"

Peter answered, "Lord, you know that I love you."

"Feed my lambs," said Jesus. Then he asked again, "Peter, do you love me?"

Peter said, "Yes, Lord, you know that I love you."

Again Jesus said, "Feed my sheep."

Then the third time Jesus said, "Peter, do you love me?"

Peter felt very bad that Jesus should ask that question three times. He knew that Jesus was thinking of the three times that Peter had denied him on the night of his trial. He answered, "Lord, you know *all* things; you know that I love you."

Jesus did know that Peter loved him. He answered, "Feed my sheep." He had a work for Peter to do, as you shall learn later.

CHAPTER 56

How Jesus Left the Earth

I Corinthians 15; Mark 16; Luke 24; Acts 1

Many times after he came out of the grave, Jesus appeared to his friends. Once when the eleven apostles were upon a mountain in Galilee, where Jesus had told them to go, he appeared to them and told them what they must do when he had gone to heaven.

He said to them, "Go and teach all nations, and baptize them in the name of the Father, and of the Son, and of the Holy Spirit. Teach them to do all things that I have commanded you. For I am with you always, even to the end of the world."

At another time Jesus appeared to five hundred of his friends who were gathered together to talk about him. Later he visited his brother, James, but the Bible does not tell us what he said.

Last of all, Jesus appeared to his disciples in Jerusalem. He went walking with them to the place they had so often visited—the village of Bethany, on the Mount of Olives.

It was now forty days since the Sunday morning on which Jesus arose from the dead. He had appeared to his friends eleven times since then. At last the time had come for him to leave the earth, and to go back to live with the Father in Heaven.

When they reached the Mount of Olives, Jesus told the disciples that they should wait in Jerusalem for the Spirit of God to come to them. "Before many days," he said, "you shall be baptized by the Holy Spirit. He will give you power that you do not have now. You must tell all the people in the world about me—those who live in Jerusalem, and in Samaria, and in the farthest parts of the earth."

These words were the last which Jesus spoke to his disciples. When he had finished telling them what he wanted them to do, he raised his hands in blessing. As they watched, they saw him rise from the ground. Higher, and higher into the blue sky he rose, till a cloud hid him from their eyes, and they saw him no more.

Wasn't that a glorious way for Jesus to go to Heaven? The disciples felt that it was. They kept looking for a long time, trying to see the last glimpse of him.

While they were still looking up into the sky, two angels dressed in white came to them. "Why do you stand looking up into Heaven?" asked the angels. "This Jesus, who has gone into Heaven, will come back again, in the same way in which you have seen him go."

The disciples knelt down and worshipped God. Then they returned to the upper room in Jerusalem where they lived together. Much of their time was spent in prayer. That was the only way they could be near to Jesus now. When they prayed, they felt that he was with them, as he had promised.

Peter said to the others, "Judas has left us, and gone to his own place. We ought to choose some other man, who has been with us all the time and who has heard and seen all that Jesus has done, to take the place of Judas. In that way we can still be twelve apostles, to tell the world about Jesus and his resurrection from the dead."

The others agreed with Peter. They chose two men, named Justus and Matthias. They prayed, "O Lord, Thou knowest the hearts of all men. Show us which one of these two men is the one that pleases Thee." And when the lots were cast, Matthias was chosen. After this, he was counted among the apostles.

Another person who spent much time with the disciples was Mary, the mother of Jesus. His brothers, too, were often with them. Like the disciples, they felt very different since Jesus had arisen from the dead.

At first, they had thought Jesus was only a man. Gradually they had begun to realize that he was also the Son of God. When he died, they were grieved and bewildered. How could the Son of God die?

But when Jesus became alive again, the happy disciples began to realize that it was God who had been with them. They knew that he could make them alive again, too. No longer were they afraid. They knew that Jesus could keep them from all harm.

CHAPTER 57

Power From Above

LUKE 24; ACTS 2

Since Jesus was gone to Heaven, the disciples spent much time in the Temple, worshipping God and praying. One day, when they were all together in one place, they suddenly heard a sound like a mighty rushing wind. It seemed to fill the room where they were. And upon the head of each disciple there appeared something that looked like a little flame of fire.

People in Jerusalem heard the strange sound and came running. It was early in the morning—only nine o'clock—but a crowd of people soon gathered around the disciples, wondering what had happened, and wondering at the strange little flames of fire.

Meanwhile the disciples felt that a wonderful change had come to them. They felt new strength and power. For the Holy Spirit had come, according to Jesus' promise. The little flames upon their heads were a sign that the Holy Spirit was in their hearts.

The power of the Holy Spirit at once made the disciples strong and brave. And now they were able to speak in languages they had not known before. They were also eager to talk, eager to tell about Jesus. And they began to talk in many different languages, telling the works of God.

The crowd listened in astonishment. They said, "Are these men not Galileans? How is it then that we hear them speak in our different languages?"

It was not strange that the men marveled. In the crowd there were people from more than a dozen different lands. There were men from the east, from the countries near Persia. There were others from

Egypt and the desert. There were men from the north, and some from far-away Rome. Each of them heard the apostles talking in his own language.

In every crowd, there are some people who can think of something disagreeable to say. In this crowd they said, "Oh, these people are drunk. That is all that is the matter with them."

But Peter stood up boldly and spoke to them.

Peter had changed since the night when he said three times that he did not know Jesus. He was no longer afraid of being killed. He was never again going to be afraid to stand up for Jesus. Peter had become the boldest of all the disciples, their leader. He was going to fight for Jesus. He really would be glad to die for his Master, to show his love.

He said to the crowd, "You men of Judea and Jerusalem, listen to me. These men are not drunk, as you seem to think. This was prophesied long ago in the Bible by the prophet Joel, in these words: *And it shall be in the last days, saith God, I will pour forth of my Spirit upon all flesh: And your sons and your daughters shall prophesy . . . And it shall be, that whosoever shall call on the name of the Lord shall be saved.*

"Now," said Peter, "this prophecy has come true. The Spirit of the Lord is being poured out upon us now. Listen to what I tell you:

"You know that Jesus of Nazareth was a man to whom God gave the power to do wonderful miracles. According to God's plan you have taken him, and you have wickedly crucified him. But God raised him up, because death could not hold him. We know that he is living, because we all saw him.

"Now he is on the right hand of God in Heaven. It is he who has sent this Holy Spirit, whose sign you see on our heads, and which makes us able to speak in other languages. Therefore you must know that God has made that same Jesus, whom you crucified, both Lord and Christ."

When the crowd heard these sure and brave words, they were troubled. They began to fear that God would punish them for their sin in killing Jesus. "Men and brethren, what shall we do?" they asked.

Peter said to them, "Be sorry for your sins, and be baptized, every one of you, in the name of Jesus Christ. God will forgive you, and will give you the Holy Spirit. Save yourselves!"

Peter and the other apostles began to baptize those who said they were sorry for their sins. All day long they baptized, and taught the people about Jesus.

At the beginning of the day there had been only about one hundred twenty followers of Jesus in the city. At the end of the day, how many do you think there were? More than three thousand!

Every day after that, the disciples preached about Jesus in the Temple and in the streets of Jerusalem. They wanted to teach everyone about Jesus, as he had told them to do while he was still on earth. And every day God added more people to the church through their preaching.

Among these believers there was a spirit of love. Nobody called anything his own, for they all sold whatever they had and shared the money with the rest. As Jesus had commanded his disciples, they often ate bread and drank wine in remembrance of his death.

This was the beginning of the Christian church. Since then, the story of Jesus has been told in nearly every land, and his followers have become a crowd that cannot be numbered.

CHAPTER 58

The Lame Man in the Temple

ACTS 3, 4

One afternoon at three o'clock, Peter and John went together to the Temple. At the place called the Beautiful Gate, where people went into the Temple, a poor lame man was lying on a rug.

This poor cripple had never walked in his whole life. He was helpless. Every day some of his friends carried him to the Beautiful Gate of the Temple. People who pitied him sometimes gave him a little money to pay for his food and clothes.

When this poor man saw Peter and John coming into the Temple, he begged them to give him something.

The two men stopped beside him. Peter said, "Look at us." The man looked up at them, thinking they were going to give him some money. Peter said, "I have no money to give you, but I have something else." He took hold of the man's hand and lifted him up, and said in a loud voice, "In the name of Jesus Christ of Nazareth, rise up and walk."

Immediately the man's feet and ankle bones became strong, and he stood up. He walked with the apostles into the Temple, running and jumping up and down in his delight, and shouting, "God be praised, God be praised, I can walk!"

The people in the Temple heard the shouting, and they ran to see what the noise was. There was the man whom they had seen at the Gate, who had never been able to walk a step. He was jumping and running and shouting, "God be praised, I can walk!"

"How did it happen?" everyone was asking. "Who healed you?"

When Peter saw the crowd gathering, he said, in a voice loud enough to be heard by all, 'Why do you all look at us as if we had cured this man by our own power? In this man God has glorified His servant, Jesus. You brought Jesus to Pilate, and would not permit Pilate to let Jesus go. You asked the governor to give you a murderer instead. You killed the Prince of life. But God made him alive again. We *saw* him. Through faith in the name of Jesus this man has become well and strong."

Then Peter changed his tone and said gently, "I know that you did not know these things. Repent and be sorry, and God will forget your sins. Some day Jesus will come again from Heaven. Long ago, God told Moses that He was going to send Jesus, and that everyone who would not listen to him would be punished. Turn away from your sins, and God will bless you."

For days the chief priests had watched crowds in the Temple flock to hear the teaching of the apostles. "This is very bad," they said.

"When we killed Jesus, we thought that would be the end. But here all these men are preaching about him, saying that he is alive. We must do something to stop it."

Soldiers were sent to arrest Peter and John and put them in jail for the night. But the words which had been preached could not be stopped. More and more people turned to Jesus, and they in turn told their friends about him. There were already about five thousand people in Jerusalem who had been baptized in his name, not even two months after Jesus had gone to Heaven.

The morning after Peter and John were thrown into prison, the chief priests gathered their friends together. The rulers, the elders, the scribes, Annas the high priest, and Caiaphas, and other Jews met to talk to Peter and John.

The two apostles were brought out of jail and set in the midst of them. "Where did you get the power to cure this man?" asked the rulers.

Peter's heart was filled with the Holy Spirit and he spoke stirringly, saying, "O rulers and elders, if you ask us how we cured the lame man, we will tell you that it was by the power of Jesus Christ of Nazareth, whom you crucified, and whom God raised from the dead. There is no other way to be saved except by Jesus."

How bold Peter had become! He was no longer afraid to die for his Lord.

The priests, who were well educated, were surprised to hear Peter and John speak so boldly, for they were ignorant men who had not been to school. Although the rulers thought themselves so wise, they did not know how to answer these ignorant men. They knew that Peter and John must have been taught by Jesus. The man who had been healed stood before them, and they could not deny that he had been made well by some miracle.

The rulers commanded Peter and John to leave the room for a few minutes, so that they could talk among themselves. "What shall we do with these men?" they said. "It is plain that they have done a won-derful miracle, and we cannot say that they have not. But this teaching must not spread. We will tell them that they must not speak about Jesus to anyone. If they do, we will punish them."

So Peter and John were brought back and were told not to speak about Jesus again. Peter was not afraid. He said, "Do you think we ought to obey you, or God? We cannot help speaking about the things that we have seen and heard."

The high priests did not know what to do. They did not dare to punish Peter and John for fear of the people. A crowd had gathered when the news spread that the high priests had arrested Peter and John. Everybody was praising God because the crippled man had been healed.

After another warning the apostles were freed. They hurried to the other believers and told them what had happened. All the company began to pray, "Lord, see how the rulers are threatening us! Help us not to be afraid, and to speak boldly. And now, Lord, give us power to work signs by the name of Thy Holy Servant, Jesus."

While they prayed, the house was shaken. They were filled with the Spirit of God, and praised the Lord.

CHAPTER 59

The Story of a Lie

ACTS 5

Among the first members of Christ's church there was a spirit of love. They lived like a big family, loving each other and taking care of each other. None of them was rich and none was poor, because they shared everything. Those who had been rich sold their houses and lands and gave the money to the apostles, who gave it to those who were needy. They felt that the things they had were not theirs, but God's, and that they must live together as children of God.

The Holy Spirit came into the hearts of the people and filled them with love. The apostles were given the power to so preach about Jesus that many who heard them believed.

Among the believers was a man named Ananias and his wife, Sapphira. They saw all the Christians selling their land, and bringing the money to Peter. They wanted everyone to think that they were just as generous. But at the same time, they did not want to give all their money away.

So when Ananias and his wife sold some land which belonged to them, they brought Peter not all the money which was given to them, but only a part. That was all right, of course. They did not have to sell the land at all. And if they did sell it, they did not have to give the money to Peter for the poor. They could have kept it all if they had wanted to.

The wrong thing was that Ananias and his wife agreed to tell a lie. When Ananias brought the money to Peter, he said that he was giving all the money for which the land had been sold.

The Holy Spirit in Peter's heart told him that this was a lie, and that Ananias had kept a part of the money for himself. It was a dreadful thing that there was a liar in the church of Jesus Christ, among all the believers who were filled with the Spirit of God.

Peter said sternly, "Ananias, why has Satan come into your heart, and told you to tell a lie? No one made you sell the land. After you sold it, the money was your own. You could have kept it all, if you had wanted to. But you are trying to deceive. You are telling a lie to God, not to me."

As Peter spoke, God punished the liar. He fell down dead at Peter's feet. Some of the young men took up the body and wrapped it in linen cloth. They carried Ananias out to bury him.

About two hours later, the wife of Ananias came in. She did not know that her husband was dead. Peter said to her, "Tell me, did you sell the land for this money which your husband brought to us?"

Sapphira had agreed beforehand with her husband to tell the lie. "Yes," she said to Peter. "We sold the land for just that amount of money which my husband brought."

Peter said, "How is it that you and your husband have agreed together to tell a lie about the price of the land? The young men are just coming back after burying your husband. They will carry you out and bury you, too."

As Peter spoke, Sapphira fell down dead. The young men came in. They saw her lying there dead at Peter's feet, and took her out, and buried her by her husband.

God sent a swift punishment to warn the people that they must not do wicked things. It taught them that God knows what we do.

CHAPTER 60

The Open Prison Doors

ACTS 5

By the power of the Holy Spirit, all the apostles were able to work miracles and to heal people as Jesus had done. Those who had sick friends brought them on beds and couches into the streets, so that the shadow of Peter might fall upon them as he went by; and they were made well.

Every day the apostles preached to the people. Those who believed talked to their friends and neighbors and brought them to the Lord.

As more people believed, the high priests became more and more angry and alarmed. At last they sent some soldiers to arrest the twelve apostles and put them in prison.

That night the angel of the Lord came down from Heaven and opened the prison doors, and let the twelve men out. The angel said,

"Go and speak in the Temple to all the people, and tell them about Jesus."

So, early in the morning, the twelve went back to the Temple and began to talk to the people. They had no need to be afraid of the priests. They knew that God would send His angels to rescue them if they should need help.

When the soldiers came to the prison that morning, they found the doors locked and the keepers still standing outside, watching. How astonished they were when they unlocked the doors and found nobody inside!

The soldiers hurried to the priests and told the strange news. "But how could they have escaped through locked doors?" asked the priests. "Why didn't the watchmen see them?"

Just then somebody came up and said, "Those men that you shut in prison last night are standing in the Temple teaching the people." The priests were more astonished than before. How did these men dare to go on talking about Jesus after they had been thrown into prison?

The captain and some officers went to the Temple to arrest the apostles again and bring them to the high priests. The soldiers did not treat the twelve roughly, for they were afraid that the people would be angry.

When Peter and the others were brought to him, the high priest asked, "Did we not command you very strictly not to teach any more in the name of Jesus? Now you are filling the city with your teaching and blaming us for killing him."

Peter answered, "We ought to obey God, rather than men. God brought Jesus into the world, but you killed him on the cross. God has set him at His right hand in Heaven. He is a Prince and a Savior. He will make his people Israel sorry for their sins, and he will forgive them. God has sent the Holy Spirit into the hearts of all who believe, so that they may teach about Jesus."

These words made the rulers furious. They knew that they had killed Jesus, but they were angry because Peter called them murderers. They said to one another, "We will have to kill these men. That is the only way to stop their teaching."

Among them was a wise man named Gamaliel, who said, "Put these men out of the room for a few minutes." When they were gone, Gamaliel said, "You must be careful what you do. You remember that about thirty-five years ago there was a man who gathered about four hundred followers and pretended he was important. Soon he was killed and his followers were scattered. After that, many people followed a man named Judas. But he also died. Let these men alone. If this teaching is from men, it will come to nothing. But if it is of God, you cannot overthrow it. If you try to, you will be fighting against God."

The rulers saw at once that this was wise advice. They decided to let the apostles live. But before letting them go, they had their servants beat the men as they had beaten Jesus. After warning them not to talk again of Jesus, the rulers let them go.

The apostles went out. Their backs were sore and bleeding, but their hearts were full of a great happiness. They were happy—not because the rulers had let them go, but because they had been beaten. They had suffered for their dear Lord, who had done so much for them.

They did not obey the rulers who told them not to speak of Jesus. Rather, they obeyed the angel who had told them to teach in the Temple. And every day more people believed.

CHAPTER 61

The Man Who Looked Into Heaven

ACTS 6, 7

Although the high priest and the rulers hated the name of Jesus, yet among the believers were some priests. They had not dared to follow him while he was still alive. When he died and rose again, they knew that this must be the Son of God.

In the church were many poor people. Some of them were old ladies whose husbands were dead, and who could not earn money. Every day the apostles gathered these people together and gave them some money or food. The rich shared what they had with the poor, and no one was in need.

As more people joined the church, there came to be so many poor that the twelve apostles were not able to take care of them and preach too. And so the apostles said to the believers, "It is better for you to choose seven good men to do this, while we give all our time to teaching."

When the seven men were chosen, the apostles laid their hands on their heads and prayed. These seven spent their time helping the poor with food and money.

One of these men was Stephen. He taught and did miracles among the people, for his heart was filled with the Holy Spirit.

One day as Stephen was teaching, some men began to argue with him. They did not want to believe, but he spoke with such wisdom that they could not prove him wrong. As they talked they became very angry, and found fault with Stephen.

At last Stephen's enemies told lies about him, saying that he spoke against Moses and against God. They stirred up the people and the scribes, and came upon Stephen suddenly with a mob. They took him before the rulers, saying, "We have heard this man speak against Moses and against God."

The rulers turned their eyes towards Stephen. They were amazed, for his face had a look of glory. It was like the face of an angel.

The high priest said to Stephen, "Are the things which these men say true?"

Then Stephen spoke, "Men, brethren, and fathers, listen to me." And he told them how God had helped their fathers long ago. He reminded them how they had refused many times to listen to God and to obey Him. They had left God and had turned to worship idols. They had killed the prophets who had told about the coming of Christ. And when Christ came, they killed him. "You have always resisted God, just as your fathers did," said Stephen.

All this was true. These Jews had killed Jesus, even as their fathers had killed God's prophets. But the rulers and the mob only grew the more angry. They shook their fists at Stephen and yelled in a rage.

Stephen lifted his eyes and looked straight into Heaven. He called out, "I see the heavens opened, and Jesus standing at the right hand of God!"

The angry mob would not listen. Yelling and raging, they ran at Stephen. They pushed and pulled him out of the city. They threw stones at him. So as to be able to throw more easily, some of them jerked off their coats and dropped them at the feet of a young man named Saul.

When Stephen knew that he was going to die, he raised his eyes to heaven and called, "Lord Jesus, receive my spirit." As the stones came thick and fast, he kneeled down. With a loud voice he cried, as Jesus had done, "Lord, lay not this sin to their charge."

Saying this, Stephen fell asleep. And he awakened in Heaven.

Stephen is called the first martyr, because he was the first one to die for love of Jesus. Since that time thousands have been killed because they loved him. Even today, in some parts of the world, Christians are hated.

As the members of the church buried the first martyr, they wept to think that so good a man had been stoned. But they knew that Stephen was happy, for he was with Christ.

CHAPTER 62

The Magician Who Tried to Buy God

ACTS 8

More and more did the Pharisees and leaders of the Jews hate the followers of Jesus. They did all they could to stop the disciples from preaching. They went into people's houses. Anyone who was found praying to Jesus or heard talking about him, was arrested and sent to prison.

Jerusalem had become a very dangerous place for the disciples. They could not talk about Jesus without danger of being arrested. Yet they could not be silent. Although the apostles stayed in Jerusalem, many other believers left the city and moved to other places. It was good that they did, for wherever they went they told people about Jesus.

One of the seven men who had been chosen to take care of the poor was called Philip. He had been a friend of Stephen, the martyr. When the rulers of Jerusalem began to arrest the believers, Philip went down to the city of Samaria and taught the people there. He cured many sick people and worked many miracles, as Jesus had done.

The people of Samaria gladly listened to Philip, and many of them believed in Jesus.

A few years earlier, you remember, Jesus had talked to the Samaritans and they had received him. The woman who had come to draw water at the well had told her friends about him. Jesus had stayed with them for two days. Probably many of those who heard Philip remembered Jesus, and became his disciples gladly now. They were baptized as members of the church.

In this city there lived a man named Simon, who was a magician. He pretended that he was a very great man, sent by God. For a long time all the people had looked up to him, because of the magic and the tricks he could do.

This magician heard the preaching of Philip, who told the people about God. He saw Philip heal the sick, and he too believed and was baptized. He stayed with Philip.

In Jerusalem, the twelve apostles heard the good news that the Samaritans believed in Jesus. They sent Peter and John to Samaria to help Philip.

All the new believers in Samaria came together in a big meeting. Peter and John prayed that they might receive the Holy Spirit. Then, a few at a time, the new believers came before the two apostles. Peter and John laid their hands on the heads of the Samaritans, and the Holy Spirit came into their hearts.

Simon the magician looked on in wonder. He could not understand how the Holy Spirit came into the hearts of the people when Peter and John laid their hands upon their heads. He was a magician, but he had never been able to do anything like this! Simon thought it was a kind of magic, like his own tricks. He brought money to the apostles and said, "Give me this power, too, that when I lay my hands on someone's head, he may receive this Spirit."

Peter was angry. Sternly he said, "May your money perish with you! This is the gift of God. It cannot be bought with money. You are not one of Christ's followers if you think such a thing, for your heart is not right before God. Be sorry, and pray that God will forgive you this sin."

Simon was frightened. "Pray God for me," he begged, for he saw now that the power of God cannot be bought with money.

CHAPTER 63

The Black Man Who Believed

ACTS 8

After preaching the gospel in many cities of the Samaritans, the disciples went back to Jerusalem. Philip did not go with them, for the angel of the Lord spoke to him and said, "Arise and go towards the south, to the road which goes down from Jerusalem to Gaza, through the desert."

Leaving Samaria, Philip went toward the south, on the road to Gaza. All around him was lonely desert country. He did not know why the Lord had sent him here, but he walked along willingly.

What should Philip see before long, but a fine chariot, drawn by two handsome horses in shining harness! In the chariot a black man was sitting, reading aloud to himself. In the front of the chariot stood his black servant, driving the horses.

This man had come from Africa, where the black people have lived since the time of Noah, and where many of them still are. His home was in Ethiopia, which is a country in Africa far away from the land of the Jews. He was very rich, for he was an important officer in the court of the queen of Ethiopia. He had charge of all her treasure— her gold and silver and jewels.

The book which this man was reading as he rode through the desert was part of the Old Testament, which he had bought in one of the shops of Jerusalem. It was the book of the prophet Isaiah.

This black man was not a worshipper of idols, like most of the people in Africa. Somehow he had learned something about the true God, and had gone to Jerusalem to worship in the Temple. Now he was reading some of the prophecies and trying to understand them.

The Spirit of God said to Philip, "Go and join this man in the chariot."

As Philip ran near the man, he heard him reading from the book of the prophet Isaiah. "Do you understand what you are reading about?" Philip asked.

"How can I, unless someone will explain it to me?" answered the black man. "Come up into the chariot and tell me what it means."

So Philip climbed into the chariot. The place where the man was reading was the seventh verse of the fifty-third chapter of Isaiah, which tells about Christ: *He was led as a sheep to the slaughter, and as a lamb before his shearer is dumb, so he openeth not his mouth.* The black man said, "I do not understand this. Is the prophet saying it about himself, or about some other man?"

Then Philip explained that Isaiah prophesied about Christ and his death. He told all about Jesus and about the wonderful things that had happened.

As they rode along, they came to a small pool or stream. The man said to Philip, "Here is some water. Why may I not be baptized?"

So the black man commanded the chariot to stand still. Philip went down with him and stood in the water, and baptized him, in the name of the Father, and the Son, and the Holy Spirit.

As they came up out of the water, the Spirit of the Lord took Philip away, and the black man did not see him again. He went on down the road, very happy. When he reached his home, he must have told all his friends about the wonderful things he had heard.

The Spirit of the Lord took Philip to the sea-shore. All along the coast Philip went, preaching to everyone he met.

The story of Jesus was spreading very far. The people who moved away from Jerusalem carried it with them wherever they went. The black man took it with him into Africa. Before long it would go still farther.

CHAPTER 64

The Light on the Road

ACTS 9, 26

Among the Pharisees was a young man named Saul. Like all the other Pharisees, Saul hated the followers of Jesus and did everything he could to make trouble for them. He had held the coats of the men who stoned Stephen and he had cheered them on, for he believed that all those who taught about Jesus were fighting against God. If he heard of people who believed in Jesus, he led soldiers into their homes and had them put in prison.

Saul's parents were Jews who lived in Tarsus, a heathen city. Because they did not want their son Saul to grow up without knowing about God, they had sent him to school in Jerusalem. At this time Jews were living in many cities outside their own land. Wherever they went they built synagogues and worshipped God just as they had done in their own country. As often as they could, they went back to Jerusalem for the feasts, and many sent their children there to school.

Saul had had a fine education in Jerusalem. His teacher had been that wise doctor of the law, Gamaliel, who had advised the Pharisees to let the Christians alone.

Saul had studied the Old Testament until he knew it very well. He was strict in keeping the law and in doing what he thought was right. He truly believed that the followers of Jesus were teaching wrong things, and that they were working against God. Saul thought it was his duty to do all he could to stop them. Because of him many believers were put in prison, and some were killed.

Even this was not enough. Saul went to the high priest and said, "We must stamp out this new religion, if we can. If you will give me letters to the priests in Damascus, I will go there. If I find any of the followers of Jesus there, I will bind them and bring them back to Jerusalem and you can put them in prison here."

So the high priest gave him some letters telling the priests in Damascus to help arrest the followers of Jesus. Saul set out, taking some men to help him in his work.

Damascus, where Saul was going, is a very interesting place, the oldest city in the world. It was founded by Uz, the great-grandson of Noah. Even today it is a big city, with one hundred fifty thousand people living in it. Damascus is more than one hundred miles away from Jerusalem. Saul must have needed several days to travel that distance, even if he and his men rode on donkeys. Probably at night they stopped at inns beside the road.

After Saul and his men had been travelling for some days, they came near the city of Damascus. Suddenly a light streamed from Heaven, brighter than the light of the sun. It was so startling and so, blinding that they all fell down to the ground.

Saul heard a voice out of Heaven saying, "Saul, Saul, why do you persecute me? It is hard for you to kick against the pricks."

Saul was very much frightened. He trembled all over as he replied, "Who is speaking to me?"

The voice said, "I am Jesus of Nazareth. I am the one against whom you are fighting."

This was a tremendous surprise to Saul. He had thought Jesus was dead! He had thought that he was doing right, and that the followers of Jesus were wrong. He had thought that God was pleased with him. Now when he heard this voice from Heaven, he knew that he had been wrong, and that he had been fighting against God.

He said very humbly, "Lord, what do you want me to do?"

Jesus answered, "Stand up, Saul. I have appeared to you to show you that after this you are not to fight against me any more. You are to become one of my disciples and tell everybody about me. I will appear to you again and show you more about myself. Go into Damascus, and there it shall be told you what you must do."

"Do you understand what you are reading?" Philip asked. Acts 8

"What I have made clean, you must not call unclean." Acts 10

From that minute Saul became a changed man. From that minute he was a follower of Jesus. But when the light disappeared and he tried to go on, he found that he could not see. He had been struck blind by the glory of that light, which was brighter than the sun.

The men with Saul had seen the light and heard a voice, but they had not understood what the voice said. They had not been blinded by the light, and so they took Saul by the hand and led him into the city.

CHAPTER 65

The Changed Man

ACTS 9

Down the streets of Damascus came a little procession. A group of men were carefully leading by the hand a well-dressed man who was blind.

The street they were walking on was called the "Straight street" because it ran through the city. The men went along until they came to the house of a man named Judas. There they went in. If you had stopped them, they would have told you a strange story about a bright light which had appeared to them as they were coming into the city, and which had blinded their companion, Saul.

For three days Saul was blind. He sat in Judas' house without talking, neither eating nor drinking. He wanted to think about what had happened.

Saul knew now that the disciples of Jesus were right, and that Jesus was really the Son of God. Like all the other Pharisees, Saul had thought that Jesus was only a man, who deserved to be killed because he said that he was God. Saul had thought the disciples were not telling the truth when they said that Jesus rose from the dead.

But now, a great change had come over Saul. He had heard Jesus speak from Heaven, and had been blinded by his glory.

Having had a very fine education in the school of the great teacher Gamaliel, Saul knew all that the Old Testament said would happen to Christ. As Saul sat quietly in his blindness, he saw that every one of those Old Testament prophecies had been fulfilled by Jesus.

In the same city lived one of Jesus' true disciples, named Ananias. This man had heard of Saul. Somebody in Jerusalem had sent word to the disciples in Damascus to warn them that Saul was coming to arrest them and throw them into prison.

One night the Lord appeared to Ananias in a vision and said to him, "Ananias."

"Yes, Lord, I am here," he said.

God said, "Get up and go to the house of Judas, who lives in Straight street, and ask to see a man named Saul, who is praying to Me. He has had a vision, in which he saw a man named Ananias coming in and putting his hands on him to cure him of his blindness."

But Ananias was afraid. He said, "Lord, I have heard such dreadful things of this man! He has done terrible things to the good disciples in Jerusalem. He has come here to arrest all who are Thy followers."

The Lord said, "You do not need to be afraid of him now, Ananias. I have chosen him to be one of My truest disciples. I have a great work for him to do. He is going to preach about Me to kings and to the heathen, and to the children of Israel. Instead of arresting My followers, he himself is going to suffer many things for My sake."

No longer was Ananias afraid. He went to see Saul and said, "Brother Saul, the Lord Jesus, who appeared to you in the way, has sent me to you, so that you might be cured of your blindness, and might also be filled with the Holy Spirit. For God chose you to be His disciple, and to see Jesus and to hear his voice, so that you can tell all men what you have seen and heard."

Ananias put his hands on Saul, and the blindness left Saul's eyes, so that he could see again. At once he was baptized in the name of the Father, and the Son, and the Holy Spirit. The man who had come to arrest the believers was a member of Christ's church!

Saul was hungry and weak and faint, for he had eaten nothing for three days. As soon as he had been given some food he felt strong and well. He was eager to go into the synagogue and begin to tell people what had happened to him.

CHAPTER 66

Saul Escapes Twice

ACTS 9

How surprised the Jews of Damascus were one morning! In wonder they listened to a man who was telling them about Jesus, the Savior. Then they turned to each other and asked, "Isn't this the very same man who came here to arrest the followers of Jesus? Isn't this man called Saul?" Many of those who listened began to believe what he was preaching.

Saul was a well educated man. When he came to believe in Jesus he became one of the greatest preachers that the world has ever known. He also wrote many of the books of the New Testament, for God told him what to say. Saul was well prepared to work for God, and many people believed on Jesus through his preaching.

(There is good reason why children should study well. God may need an educated man or woman for some great work. God has work for all of us to do, and a child is serving God when he studies to prepare for the work God has for him.)

Many of the Jews would not believe. They said that Jesus could not be the Promised One. They expected the Savior to be a king, with a great army to fight all the enemies of his people. Many Jews are looking for such a Savior today. Like those of Saul's time, they will not believe that Jesus is the Promised One.

After Saul had been preaching in Damascus for a long time, the unbelieving Jews became very angry and wanted to kill him. They watched the gate of the city day and night, so that he might not get away. It was dangerous for Saul to stay there any longer. But how could he get away while the gate was watched?

At last some of the disciples thought of a plan. They got a large, strong basket and tied ropes on the handles. One night they went to a place far away from the gate, where nobody was watching. Then they climbed on top of the high wall which surrounded the city. They let Saul down into the fields in the basket.

Saul made his way carefully through the fields. When he was far away from the city, he walked along the road towards Jerusalem, a hundred miles away. How different this journey was from his trip to Damascus! Then, he was eager to put the disciples of Jesus into prison. Now, he was fleeing to save his life because he too believed in Jesus.

When Saul reached Jerusalem he went to Peter and John and the rest of the apostles. He told them he wanted to live with them and teach about Jesus. They were afraid to receive him, because they remembered that he had arrested and killed many of their friends.

Barnabas, one of the disciples, knew about the change which had taken place in Saul's life. He told the apostles that Saul had seen Jesus on the way to Damascus, and that Jesus had spoken to him, and that Saul had earnestly preached about Jesus in Damascus. When the disciples heard this story, they gladly received Saul.

Saul lived in Jerusalem with the disciples, teaching about Jesus. Often he talked to the Greeks who lived in the city. But after a while the unbelieving Jews became very angry to hear his preaching. Like, those in Damascus, they tried to kill him.

The apostles saw that it was not safe for Saul to remain. They went with him as far as the city of Caesarea, on the seacoast. For safety he went still farther north to the city of Tarsus, where he had been born. There he lived for a while.

CHAPTER 67

The Good Woman Who Was Brought to Life

Acts 9

About forty miles away from Jerusalem was a city called Joppa. It was a large and busy place, for it had a good harbor. Ships from all over the world came there.

In this city lived many followers of Jesus. Some of them had gone there because it was not safe for them to stay in Jerusalem. They had told others about Jesus, and now in this city, as in many others, there was a group of believers.

One of the disciples was a very good lady named Dorcas. She spent her days doing good things and helping people. The poor people and the widows loved her, because she was kind to them. And when Dorcas became sick and died, all the disciples in Joppa were very sad.

It happened at that time that Peter was in a town a few miles away. He had been going to many towns, preaching about Jesus and healing the sick. The friends of Dorcas heard that Peter healed a man who had been sick and in bed for eight years. In their trouble they sent for him, and brought him to the room where Dorcas lay dead. The poor people stood there, weeping. They showed Peter the nice clothes that Dorcas had made for them.

Peter made all the people go out of the room. Kneeling down, he prayed to God to bring Dorcas back to life again. Then he turned to the bed and said, "Dorcas, arise."

Dorcas opened her eyes, as though she had only been asleep. When she saw Peter beside her, she sat up. He took her hand and helped her rise. Then he called her friends and the poor people who had been mourning for her, and showed them that she was living.

This was a miracle, like the wonderful things Jesus did on earth. Jesus had promised that the Holy Spirit would enable the disciples to do miracles, too. There was a difference between the wonderful things which Jesus did and those which Peter and the other disciples did. The wonderful works of Jesus were done by his own power, because he was the Son of God. But Peter never pretended to cure people by his own power. He always said that he healed by the power of Jesus.

After healing Dorcas, Peter stayed in Joppa for a long time. He lived with a man called Simon, a tanner. Many people in the city heard what had happened, and believed in Jesus. Peter spent his time talking about his Master. All the Jews who went to the synagogue heard him again and again.

CHAPTER 68

A Lesson Peter Had to Learn

ACTS 10

None of the followers of Jesus thought of telling the Gospel to Greeks and Romans and others who were not Jews. The Jews never had anything to do with heathen people, and they thought that the salvation of Jesus was only for themselves. The apostles had not yet learned that Jesus wanted them to go into all the world and tell all peoples about him.

Not far from Joppa, where Peter was staying, was a place called Caesarea. In this city lived a Roman soldier named Cornelius. He was a centurion, which means a captain over a hundred men.

Cornelius was probably an Italian, but although he was not a Jew he had learned to pray to the true God. He had taught his family and servants to worship God, too. And he was very generous in helping poor people.

One day, about three o'clock in the afternoon, a strange thing happened to Cornelius. While he was praying, he had a vision. An angel said to him, "Cornelius!"

The brave soldier was frightened. He asked, "What is it, Lord?"

The angel said, "God has seen your good deeds and heard your prayers. He wants you to send to Joppa for a man named Simon Peter, who lives by the seaside in the house of Simon, a tanner."

When the angel went away, Cornelius called two of his household servants and a good old soldier who lived with him. He told them what the angel had said, and sent them to bring Peter back with them.

The next day, at the time when the three servants of Cornelius finally came near Joppa, a very curious thing happened to Peter.

About noon, while the dinner was being cooked, he went up to the flat roof of the house. He was hungry and he wished the dinner were ready.

The roof-top was quiet, because it was separated from the rest of the house. There was no disturbance; and as Peter waited, he prayed.

While Peter prayed, he had a vision. He saw a great sheet let down from Heaven by the four corners, like a kind of bag. In it were all kinds of four-footed animals and wild beasts and creeping things and birds. He heard a voice saying, "Get up, Peter, and kill some of these animals and eat them."

Peter was astonished. Many hundreds of years before, in the law of Moses, God had told the people to eat only certain kinds of animals, which were called clean. Sheep and goats and cows were clean, but pigs and lions and cats and many other kinds were called unclean.

No matter how hungry a Jew was, he would not touch an unclean animal. So when Peter heard a voice saying, "Rise, Peter, kill and eat," he said, "Oh, no, Lord, for I have never eaten anything that is common or unclean."

The voice answered, "What I have made clean, you must not call unclean."

This vision came three times. After the third time the sheet went back into the sky. While Peter was wondering about it, the three men sent by Cornelius came looking for him. They stood in front of the gate and called out, "Is Simon Peter staying here."

The Holy Spirit said to Peter, "There are three men here who are looking for you. Arise and go with them. I have sent them."

Since it was late in the day, Peter asked the men to stay with him that night. In the morning he and some of his friends went with them.

Cornelius was waiting for them. He met Peter at the gate and fell down in worship. Peter pulled him quickly to his feet and said, "You must not do that, for I am only a man like yourself."

As they walked into the house, Peter was surprised to find a whole roomful of people. They were the family and friends of Cornelius. He had invited them to come and hear what Peter would say.

"You know," Peter began, "that a Jew may not visit anyone who is not a Jew. But God has showed me that I must not call any man common or unclean. I came when you sent for me, and now I would like to know why you asked me to come."

Cornelius answered, "Four days ago, as I prayed, an angel in bright clothing stood beside me. He told me to send for you. I am very glad that you have come. I have invited all my friends to hear what God has told you to tell us."

"I see now," said Peter, "that God does not love only the Jews, as I always thought. Now I know that in every nation, God loves those who love Him and try to please Him." He went on and told about Jesus, who died for sinners.

As Peter spoke, the Holy Spirit came into the hearts of the people who were listening, and they began to speak in many different languages, as the apostles had done. At this sign, Peter knew that these people, too, were now the disciples of Jesus. He baptized them, and they became members of Christ's church.

At last Peter understood what Jesus meant when he said, "Go ye into *all* the world."

CHAPTER 69

A New Church

Acts 11

When the church in Caesarea had grown strong, Peter went back to Jerusalem. The disciples there found fault with him. "We heard that you went into the house of men who were not Jews, and that you ate with them," they said. "Why did you do that? You know that that is against the law of Moses."

Then Peter told them of his vision—about the sheet which came down from Heaven, and the voice which said, "What God has made clean, you must not call common." He told them about the angel which had come to Cornelius, and about the coming of the Holy Spirit into the hearts of the people in the house of Cornelius.

"If God has taken these people into His church, it was only right for me to baptize them," said Peter. God, who knows the hearts of all men, gave the Holy Spirit to them, just as He did to us. And who was I that I could stand against God?"

When the disciples heard these things, they stopped finding fault with Peter. They saw that it was God's doing. They began to rejoice, because now they understood for the first time that Jesus had come for all men. Before this, they had supposed that God wanted only the Jews, His own people, to be saved and to live with Him in Heaven.

Now they remembered that Jesus had said, "Go ye into all the world and preach the gospel to every creature." They also remembered that God had said to Abraham, "In thy seed shall all the nations of the earth be blessed."

When the disciples thought of the big world, reaching far, far away to foreign countries, they saw for the first time how wonderful it is that Jesus died to save men everywhere. They began to realize how big their work was.

You remember that, after Stephen was killed, it was not safe for the disciples to stay in Jerusalem. Some of them settled in the city of Antioch, near the sea-coast. This was a very important city. When the disciples went there, they told their new neighbors about Jesus. Many of the Greeks who lived in the city believed.

When the church in Jerusalem heard that the Greeks were turning to God, they realized that here was a chance for them to follow Jesus' command to preach. They sent a man to form a church in Antioch. This man was Barnabas, one of the very first disciples. He was one of those who sold land and gave the money to the poor. He had become a great teacher and prophet in the church. The apostles found him to be such a helper that they changed his name from Joses to Barnabas, which means *the son of consolation.*

The people at Antioch were glad to have Barnabas come to preach to them. The new church grew so fast that soon it needed two ministers. Barnabas went to Tarsus, where Saul was living, and asked him to come and help. For a whole year the two disciples stayed at Antioch.

It was at Antioch that the disciples were first called Christians, or followers of Christ. All over the world that name is given them to this day.

But while Saul and Barnabas were preaching in Antioch, things were not so happy in Jerusalem. The wicked King Herod, who was ruling the land of the Jews, had come to Jerusalem. He was the nephew of the Herod who had killed John the Baptist, and he was even more cruel than his uncle had been.

To please the unbelieving Jews, he arrested James, the brother of John, one of the three whom Jesus so specially loved. Herod had his soldiers cut off the head of James.

The unbelieving Jews were very well pleased. Now that Herod was on their side, they were sure that in a short time there would be no more Christians in the world.

CHAPTER 70

The Angel in Prison

ACTS 12

Herod saw that the Jewish leaders were pleased when he killed James. So he sent soldiers to arrest Peter, too. He put Peter into prison. He planned to keep him there until after the Feast of Unleavened Bread, and then kill him.

Once when the disciples were put in prison by the high priest, they had escaped, though all the doors were locked. Herod decided he was not going to let such a thing happen again.

He appointed sixteen soldiers to take turns guarding Peter, four at a time. To make it doubly sure, one of Peter's hands was chained to a soldier on his right side, and the other to a soldier at his left. Besides all this, the keepers of the prison stood in front of the doors day and night. "There!" laughed Herod. "I'd like to see him get away now."

And what were the other disciples doing, while Peter was in prison? They kept on praying that God would save him. Peter, too, was praying, though he was not afraid to die for Jesus.

For several days he was kept in prison. At last the feast was over. The next morning Herod was going to bring Peter out and cut off his head. That night many of the disciples met in the home of Mark, to pray that God would save Peter's life.

In the middle of the night, when all the guards were soundly sleeping, the angel of the Lord came into the prison. A light shone into the cell, but no one woke up. The angel went to Peter and touched him gently, saying very softly, "Get up quickly, Peter." At those words the chains fell from Peter's hands.

The angel said, "Put your shoes on, and dress yourself." Peter had been sound asleep, and he was not more than half awake now. He thought he must be dreaming, but he dressed himself and put on his shoes.

The angel said, "Put on your coat, and follow me."

Peter still thought it was all a dream, but he put on his coat and followed without a word. The angel led him past the first guard of the prison, and then past the second guard.

A stone wall with a big iron gate surrounded the prison. When Peter and the angel came to the locked gate, it opened all by itself and they passed through. They were outside the prison. Peter was free!

After they had walked together through one street leading away from the prison, the angel disappeared. The streets were dark and quiet. Peter stood still, wondering whether he was awake or asleep. Soon the cold night air made him wake up. He realized that he was not in prison, but in the streets of the city. And then he knew that God had sent an angel to rescue him.

Down the dark streets Peter walked till he reached the house of Mark, where a light shone. The Christians were still there praying, although it was the middle of the night. The door of the house was locked tight. In those dangerous times the disciples had to be very careful.

So when Peter came to Mark's house he knocked loudly on the gate. A young girl named Rhoda came to find out who was there in the middle of the night. She was not going to open the door to strangers, who might be thieves, or perhaps soldiers come to arrest them all. She called, "Who's there?"

Peter answered, "It is I, Peter. Open the gate for me."

Rhoda knew that it was Peter's voice. In her delight and excitement she forgot to open the gate, and left Peter standing outside. She ran into the house shouting, "It's Peter! It's Peter!"

They said, "You are crazy. Peter is in prison."

But Rhoda said, "It is Peter! I know it is!"

"Then it must be his spirit," they said.

But Peter kept on knocking. So at last some of them went to the gate. God had answered their prayers, for here was Peter, safe and sound! How glad they were to see him!

After a while, Peter beckoned to them to keep quiet. Then he told them how God had set him free. His friends fell down on their knees and thanked God, who by His almighty power had rescued Peter out of the hands of wicked Herod.

Peter knew that it would not be safe for him to stay in Jerusalem. By night he went quietly to another place, where Herod could not find him.

As soon as daylight came, there was a great stir in the prison, because no one knew what had become of Peter. His guards were just as surprised as anyone. They had not heard a sound. And the keepers on the outside had not seen anybody go out!

Herod was furiously angry when he heard that Peter had escaped. He asked the guards all sorts of questions. At last he said angrily, "I'll show them what happens to people who let my prisoners go. Cut off their heads, every one of them!"

Cruel Herod! Your time is almost over!

Soon after this Herod went to live in his own city. He became very angry with the people of two cities near by. They were afraid of him, and so they sent word that they would like to make peace.

On a certain day they came to him. Herod sat on his royal throne in all his robes, and made a speech. The people feared him and wanted to please him. "It is the voice of a god, and not of a man," they shouted.

This pleased Herod, but it displeased God. Herod had often sinned against men with his cruelty. But now he sinned against God, when he allowed people to call him a god.

At that moment the angel of the Lord struck Herod with a terrible disease. His servants had to carry him from his throne. Soon afterwards this enemy of the Christians died.

CHAPTER 71

On to Cyprus

ACTS 13

While the Christians in Jerusalem were living in fear of wicked Herod, the church in Antioch was quietly growing stronger and stronger. Through the preaching of Saul and Barnabas more and more people learned about Jesus.

You will be surprised to hear that another disciple who preached in Antioch was the foster-brother of wicked Herod. They had been brought up together, but they were not at all alike.

At this time the Holy Spirit spoke to the church at Antioch, and said, "I want Saul and Barnabas to leave this church and to go farther into other countries to preach to the heathen."

After the Christians had prayed and laid their hands on the heads of Saul and Barnabas, they sent them away. Barnabas and Saul, who was now called Paul, went to the sea-coast. There they found a ship which took them to the island of Cyprus, near Greece. On this island lived many Greeks.

The Greeks worshipped a great many gods, not one great Creator of heaven and earth. They thought that the gods were much like men, only a little stronger, and that they lived on a high mountain in the north of Greece.

To the Greeks, the greatest god was Jupiter. Another, named Mercury, had wings on his feet and could fly very swiftly. Diana was the goddess of hunters. Venus was the goddess of love and beauty. There were many others, all of them very much like ordinary men and women.

Although they worshipped many idols, the Greek people were not like the heathen tribes in Africa and other countries. They were artistic and well educated. They were famous for their schools and teachers. Some of them were so wise that even today the books they wrote are studied in our schools.

The Greeks had the most beautiful language in the world, and they wrote some of the loveliest poetry. Their artists made marble statues of their gods, shaped like beautiful men and women, which are among the greatest works of art the world has ever known.

Many of the wise Greeks knew that their gods were not true gods. They tried and tried to find out about the one true God.

But knowledge of God is something that men cannot find out for themselves. Even before the time of Abraham, God had told the Jews about Himself. If God had not told us about Himself in the Bible, we, too, would be worshipping idols.

For many centuries the Jews had lived apart from other nations, because God did not want them to forget what He told them about Himself. But after Jesus came, God wanted the disciples to go to all the nations of the world and to teach them about the true God and His Son. That was why Paul and Barnabas were sent among the Greeks.

Paul and Barnabas preached from one end of the island of Cyprus to the other. Then they went into a boat again and sailed to Perga. From there they went to another city called Antioch. This was not the place from which they had been sent, although it had the same name.

In the Jewish synagogue of Antioch Paul preached. Both Jews and Greeks came to hear him. They listened very closely. Afterwards the Jews went home, but many Greeks stayed to beg Paul to preach to them the next Sabbath day.

On the next Sabbath, almost the whole city came to hear Paul and Barnabas preach. When the Jews saw the crowds, they were angry and began to contradict what Paul and Barnabas said. Seeing this, Paul and Barnabas said, "Since you do not want to listen to our words, we will stop preaching to you, and will preach only to those who are not Jews."

The Greeks were very glad. They listened carefully, and many of them became Christians. They told their friends what Paul said about the true God, and soon all that country heard about Jesus.

Before long the jealous Jews made trouble for Paul and Barnabas, and drove them away. The two missionaries went to Iconium. There they preached in the Jewish synagogue, and many Jews and Greeks believed.

CHAPTER 72

Why People Thought Paul Was God

ACTS 14

In the synagogue of Iconium, every Sabbath day, two men got up to talk. Always they talked about the same things—about the Son of God, Jesus who had come to save his people. Many of the Jews and Greeks of the city believed what the men said, but others did not. After a while, those who did not believe began to make trouble for the missionaries. They even made a plan to stone them.

But the two preachers, Paul and Barnabas, found out about it, and they fled to the cities of Lystra and Derbe.

At Lystra there was a man who had been a cripple all his life. He had been born with deformed feet. He had never been able to walk a single step, nor even to stand up.

When this man heard Paul speak, he believed. Seeing this, Paul said to him, "Stand upright on your feet." At once the man jumped up. He stood without falling, and even walked.

Then the people of the city could not believe that Paul and Barnabas were men, like themselves. They thought that they must be gods come down to earth in the form of men, for they believed that their gods often came to earth. And no man could heal a cripple!

Barnabas they called Jupiter; and Paul they called Mercury, because he did most of the talking. They started to worship Paul and

Barnabas and to offer sacrifices to them. The priests of Jupiter brought some wreaths of flowers and some oxen for burnt offerings.

But as soon as the two disciples heard about this, they ran among the people and called out, "Sirs, do not do this. We are men like yourselves. We have come here to tell you to turn away from such foolish-, ness. Turn away from idols, and believe in the true God, who made heaven and earth, and all things that are in them."

But in spite of all that Paul and Barnabas said, they could hardly keep the people from offering sacrifices.

Later, some of the same Jews who had wanted to stone Paul at Iconium came to this city. They told the people bad and untrue things about Paul and Barnabas. The people changed their minds, and decided that the two men were not gods, but mischief makers. They threw stones at Paul, whom they had wanted to worship. Finally, when they thought he was dead, they dragged his body out of the city into the fields, and went away.

Some of the Christians were weeping to see Paul treated so cruelly. They went over to him very lovingly, and found to their surprise that he was still breathing, although he had seemed to be dead. After a little while Paul opened his eyes. Though he was sore and bruised, he was able to get up and go to the house where he had stayed.

The next day he and Barnabas left Lystra and went to Derbe. There they preached the gospel and were happy to find that many people believed. Then they went back and visited all the places where they had preached before.

They had started a church in each of these cities, and now when they returned they appointed elders in each church.

At last Paul and Barnabas got into a ship and sailed back to Antioch, to the church that had sent them out. The disciples there called a meeting of all the Christians in that city, to listen to what Paul and Barnabas had to say about their missionary journey, and how God had turned many heathen to Jesus.

Paul and Barnabas stayed a long time—perhaps six or seven years —and preached to the church in Antioch.

The two largest churches were the one in Jerusalem, of which James the brother of Jesus was head, and the one in Antioch. But small churches were springing up everywhere, in all countries.

CHAPTER 73

A New Journey

Acts 15, 16

A few years after the first missionary journey, Paul said to his friend Barnabas, "Let us make another journey, and visit all the new churches to see how they are getting along."

Barnabas wanted to take with them a young man named Mark. Paul said, "We took him the first time, but he did not stay with us very long. He soon turned back. I don't think we ought to take him again."

They could not reach an agreement. Barnabas wanted to take Mark, but Paul could not believe that it would be wise to choose a companion who might again turn back on the way.

At last they separated. Barnabas took Mark with him, and sailed to the island of Cyprus. Paul chose Silas to go with him. They did not go to Cyprus. Instead of travelling by sea, as Paul had done before, they went by land across the mountains.

Soon Paul and Silas reached Derbe and Lystra, where churches had been founded on the first visit. One of the Christians here was a fine young man named Timothy. His father was a Greek, but his mother and his grandmother were Jews. They were good women, and had taught Timothy to love God. Even "from the time he was a child, he had known the Scriptures."

Paul loved this young man as if he had been his own son. He invited Timothy to go with him and Silas as helper on their missionary trip, and Timothy was glad to join them.

Preaching everywhere they went, the three missionaries travelled throughout the cities of that country. At last they came to Troas, a city on the sea-shore. While they were here, Paul had a vision one night. It seemed to him that he saw a man standing before him, saying, "Come over into Macedonia and help us." Paul knew that the vision had been sent because the Lord wanted him to go to preach in a new country, to people who had never heard of Jesus.

Macedonia is a large country north of Greece, separated from Troas by a sea. The missionaries found a ship which would take them to the new land. For several days they sailed. At last they came to the big city of Philippi. There they stayed for a few days.

Paul and his helpers were now completely surrounded by heathen people who worshipped idols. It seemed that there were not enough Jews in the city to build a synagogue.

When the Sabbath day came Paul had no synagogue to preach in. There was a place by the river where the people used to go and pray. Some women were gathered there. The missionaries sat down and talked to them about Jesus Christ.

One of these women was a seller of purple dyes, named Lydia. She was a true worshipper of God; and when she heard the things Paul said about the Son of God, her heart was opened. She invited the three men to stay in her house.

CHAPTER 74

The Poor Fortune-Teller

ACTS 16

In the city where Paul and Silas were preaching, there was a young woman who was a fortune-teller. She was not in her right mind, for an evil spirit lived in her and made her tell things about the future. Many people believed that what she said was sure to happen. They asked her all sorts of questions about the future, and did whatever she told them.

Some men of the city had made this poor girl their slave. Every day she had to go out into the streets to tell people's fortunes for money. Her masters had become rich through the money she brought back to them.

Whenever she saw **Paul** and **Silas** and **Timothy** in the streets, the poor girl followed after them, calling out so that everybody could hear, "These men are the servants of the most high God, and they come to tell us how to be saved."

Of course people stared, to see the young girl following three strangers. Everybody knew that she was not in her right mind. Those who did not believe in her fortune-telling laughed at the sight.

Paul did not like this at all. He knew that it was an evil spirit which spoke through the lips of the poor girl. And he did not want people to laugh at his teaching.

For many days the girl followed the missionaries, calling out after them. At last **Paul** turned and said to the evil spirit that was in her, "I command thee in the name of Jesus Christ, to come out of her."

Immediately the evil spirit came out of her, and the girl was in her right mind. But now that the spirit had left her, she could not tell fortunes any more. When her masters found this out, they were very angry with Paul and Silas. They did not care about the poor girl. They were not glad that she was well and happy. All they cared about was the money she had brought them by telling fortunes.

"We don't want strangers to come and interfere with our business," they said furiously. "We won't put up with it." Dragging Paul and Silas before the rulers of the city they complained, "These men do not belong here. They are Jews, and they disturb our city. They teach customs which it is not lawful for us to follow. We do not want to follow Jewish customs. We are Romans, and we want to follow Roman customs."

As the men talked, they aroused the people in the market place. Even the rulers became so angry that they tore their clothes and commanded that Paul and Silas be beaten.

So the prisoners were dragged off to the public whipping place and bound to a post. They were given a terrible beating with a cruel knotted whip.

After the beating, Paul and Silas were cast into prison and the jailor was warned to keep them safely. Their feet were fastened together in a wooden frame called the stocks, which held them so tightly that they could not take a single step. They could not even change their uncomfortable position, because their feet were held straight in front of them.

Poor Paul and Silas! Their backs were swollen and bleeding and smarting with pain. As night came, the prison grew dark. Paul and Silas could not sleep because of their pain. They could not even lie down, but had to sit with their feet straight out in front of them.

But when they remembered that they were suffering for Jesus, who had borne so much more for them, their souls were happy in spite of their pain. They lifted up their voices and sang songs of praise to God and prayed. The other prisoners listened in wonder. Who were these strange men, who could sing even after they were beaten and thrown into prison?

CHAPTER 75

The Jailor Who Believed

ACTS 16

Although Paul and Silas had been thrown into prison for helping the poor girl, God had not forgotten them. He was taking care of them, just as He had taken care of Peter in prison in Jerusalem. His almighty power is far greater than any jailor's. No prison door in the world can remain closed against it.

About midnight, when Paul and Silas were singing, suddenly there was a great earthquake. Everything began to rock. The very foundations of the prison were shaken, and all the doors flew open. The stocks fell apart, and the prisoners found that their chains were broken. They were free!

The great earthquake wakened the keeper of the prison. When he saw that all the prison doors were open, he thought that all the prisoners had escaped. He knew that if they got away, he would be punished cruelly. The rulers would surely kill him.

The jailor was a heathen, and he had never heard the commandment that we know so well, "Thou shalt not kill." He thought it would be better to kill himself than to be put to death by the rulers because the prisoners had escaped.

Drawing his sword, he was ready to drive it into his heart, when Paul cried out to him, "Do not kill yourself, for we are all here. No one has run away."

When the jailor heard these words, he called to someone to bring him a light, and he ran into the prison. Trembling and humble, he fell down before Paul and Silas, begging them to come out of the prison into his house. He felt that Paul and Silas must be servants of God, since they were such good men that they would not run away when they had a chance to do so. They must know the truth about God. "Sirs, what must I do to be saved?" he asked.

They said to him, "Believe on the Lord Jesus Christ, and you shall be saved, and all the members of your household too."

Probably the jailor did not even know who Jesus Christ was. But Paul and Silas explained that Jesus Christ was the Son of the true God, who had come down into the world to die on the cross for the sins of the world, and who had risen the third day and was now in heaven at God's right hand.

While the jailor was listening, all his household had gathered to hear these words of life. The jailor, his wife and children, and all his servants were baptized that night, and there was great happiness in the household of the jailor.

Then the jailor brought cool water and carefully washed the ugly cuts where Paul and Silas had been so cruelly beaten. He told his servants to bring some nice food. The two prisoners were very hungry, for they had not eaten anything for a long time.

When morning came, the rulers who had thrown Paul and Silas into prison sent word to the jailor to let them go. But instead of leaving at once, as most prisoners are glad to do, Paul and Silas stayed there. They had been very badly treated, although they had done nothing wrong. Without a trial, they had been punished; and this was against the law.

In those days there were certain cities in different parts of the world which were called Roman cities, although they were not in Italy. All the people who were born in these cities were called Romans, and they had many privileges which other people did not have. Sometimes rich men paid a great deal of money for the privilege of being called a Roman citizen. No Roman citizen could be beaten or put into prison unless he had first been tried and found guilty.

Now Tarsus, where Paul was born, was one of these Roman cities, and he was therefore a Roman citizen. The rulers of Philippi thought Paul had no more right than any other Jew. They did not dream that they had broken the law by having him beaten and cast into prison.

But when the rulers sent word that Paul and Silas might go, Paul said, "They have beaten us openly without any trial, although we are

Romans. They have cast us into prison. And now do they send word to us to go out quietly and secretly? They have broken the law by putting us into prison and beating us. If they want us to go out, they themselves must come and bring us out publicly."

When the rulers heard that Paul and Silas were Romans, they were terrified. They hurried down to the jail and begged Paul and Silas to forgive them, to come out and leave their city.

So Paul and Silas went back to Lydia's house. They called all the Christians together and told them that they were going to leave Philippi. After comforting them, they left the city.

For a long time the two missionaries had lived in Philippi. A few years later, Paul wrote a letter to the church there, where he had so many friends. You will find that letter in your Bible.

CHAPTER 76

From City to City

ACTS 17

After the rulers had asked Paul and Silas to leave Philippi, the missionaries went to some other cities in Macedonia. At last they came to Thessalonica. They lived in the house of a man named Jason.

In that city there was a synagogue of the Jews. Paul and Silas went there to preach on the Sabbath day, instead of preaching on the street or by the river, as they did in many of the heathen cities.

For three Sabbath days they preached in the Jewish synagogue. Many people came to hear Paul—not only Jews, but also Greeks. A great number of Greeks were glad to hear of the true God, and of Jesus Christ, who loved them. When they heard the story of Jesus who suffered and died for the sins of the whole world, and rose again and ascended to heaven, they were glad to turn away from the idols which were made by men's hands.

But there were some of the Jews in the city who did not believe Paul's preaching. They were angry to see so many people listening to him.

Some of the rough fellows of the town gathered together in a mob. They shouted and yelled, and made such a noise that they set the city in an uproar. They came to the house of Jason, and tried to get hold of Paul and Silas and Timothy.

But the three missionaries were not in the house just then. Not finding them, the mob took Jason and some other Christians before the rulers of the city. "These men, that have turned the world upside down, have come here now," they cried. "Jason has taken them into his house. They do things against our Emperor Caesar, and they say that there is another king, named Jesus."

The rulers saw that they must calm this mob of rough fellows who were making such a noise. They made Jason and the others promise not to make any trouble, and then let them go. Since Paul and Silas and Timothy had not been found, nothing was done to them.

The Christians knew it would not be safe for Paul and his friends to stay in that place. They sent them away by night to Berea. The people of this city were more noble than those of Thessalonica. They listened to Paul very gladly, searching the scriptures every day to see if the things which Paul was telling them about Christ had been foretold by the prophets long ago.

A great many Greeks of Berea, both men and women, turned from their idols to the living God. But when the troublesome Jews of Thessalonica heard that Paul was preaching in this near-by city, they came and stirred up the people. Paul's friends thought it would be better for him to leave.

CHAPTER 77

About the Unknown God

ACTS 17

This time Paul went to Athens.

You probably know that Athens is the greatest city of Greece. It is big and beautiful, but in Paul's time it was even more splendid than it is now. It was filled with grand marble temples, in which the people worshipped. The Greeks made marble statues of their gods. Some of the statues which once stood in Greek temples were found many years later. You will find copies and pictures of them all over the world, for many people believe that they are the most beautiful statues ever made.

When Paul walked through the beautiful city and saw these idols on every hand, he knew that the people had no knowledge of the true God. He was very sorry for them, and he wanted to tell them about Jesus. At last he came to the Jewish synagogue. Although Athens was a Greek city, there were many Jews and people of other nations living in it.

Paul went into the synagogue and began to talk with the Jews who came there. Every day after that he went into the market place and preached to all who would listen to him.

The people of the city liked to hear about new ideas. In Athens lived some of the wisest men that the world has known. They spent their time teaching in the streets and the market place. It was no new thing for the people to hear men talking on the street corners.

The wise men of the city came to see Paul and to hear what he was teaching. Some of them asked, "What will this babbler say?" Others, who heard him speak of Jesus and the resurrection, said, "He seems to be teaching about strange gods."

The people were so much interested in what Paul was saying, that they brought him to the hill of Mars, where they could listen to him without interruption from the buying and selling that was going on in the market place. They asked him politely, "Will you tell us about this new doctrine which you are preaching? For you bring strange things to our ears, and we would like to know what these things mean."

So Paul stood on Mars' hill and said to them, "Ye men of Athens, I see that you are very religious. For as I passed through your city and saw the gods that you worship, I found one altar that said, *To the unknown God.* You are worshipping one god that you do not know. That is the God that I am preaching about.

"He is the God that made the world and all the things that are in the world. Because He is the Lord of Heaven and earth He does not need to live in temples that are made with men's hands. He does not need to have us give Him food or any of the things which you sacrifice to your idols. For He is the one who gives life and breath and all things to us. He wants us to seek Him, though He is not far from any of us.

"Some of your own poets have said, 'We are the children of God.' If we are the children of God, we ought not to think that God is an idol made by men, of stone or gold or silver. In the past you did not know any better, but now God wants everyone to repent of his sins. He has chosen Jesus Christ to judge the world one day, and He has given you sure proof by raising Jesus from the dead."

When Paul began to speak of the dead becoming alive again, some of the people began to mock because they did not believe that such a thing could ever happen. But others said, "We want to hear more of this doctrine." And some of them believed.

Leaving Athens, Paul came to Corinth, another city of Greece. He stayed there about two years, living with a Jew named Aquila and his wife Priscilla. Together they made tents. And on every Sabbath Day Paul preached to Jews and Greeks about the Christ.

Several years later, Paul wrote two letters to the Christians of Corinth. These letters became part of the New Testament and are called First and Second Corinthians.

From Corinth, Paul went to Ephesus. But he did not stay there. He wanted to go to Jerusalem. So he promised that he would come back, if it should be God's will, and he sailed away. He stopped at many of the new little churches, to visit them and strengthen them.

CHAPTER 78

The Riot of the Statue-Makers

Acts 19

Paul kept his promise and went back to Ephesus after a while. This time he stayed for at least two years. He founded a church there. And God performed many miracles through Paul, healing many sick and casting out many evil spirits. The church of Ephesus grew strong and big.

In that city there was a splendid temple of Diana, the goddess of hunting. And in the temple was a great statue of Diana. The people of the city thought that the statue had not been made by men, but had fallen down from heaven. Through all the country, the temple of Diana was famous, and many people came to worship there. Before going home again, many of them bought a little silver statue or image of Diana to take back with them.

One of the men who made these little images was called Demetrius. He and the other men who were in the same business were becoming very rich, for all the people thought they ought to have a statue of their goddess in their homes.

But Demetrius saw that if Paul went on preaching that the idols were not gods at all, pretty soon nobody would want to buy his images. So he called a meeting of all the men who made statues and said to them, "You know that we get our wealth by making these images. You see and hear that not only in Ephesus, but almost throughout all Asia (Asia Minor) this Paul has been telling people that idols that are made with hands are not really gods. If this goes on, soon nobody will want to buy images of Diana. Before long the temple of the goddess will be laughed at, although Asia and the world worship her now."

The silver workers were excited by this speech and they cried out in great anger, "Great is Diana of the Ephesians!"

They made such a noise with their shouting that soon the whole city was filled with confusion. The mob caught some of Paul's companions and rushed into the theater. Paul wanted to go into the theater too, but some of his friends held him back, for they were afraid that he might be injured.

In the theater there was a great crowd, some shouting one thing and some another. Most of them did not know what all the noise was about.

A man called Alexander came up to the platform and tried to talk to the people. He motioned with his hand to make them keep quiet, but when the crowd saw that he was a Jew they would not listen for fear that he would say something against their great goddess Diana. They lifted up their voices, and for almost two hours they shrieked and screamed, *"Great is Diana of the Ephesians! Great is Diana of the Ephesians!* GREAT IS DIANA OF THE EPHESIANS!"

After they had yelled their throats hoarse, the town officer managed to get them quiet. When they could hear him talk he said to them, "You men of Ephesus, who does not know that the city of Ephesus contains the temple of the great goddess Diana, and the image which fell down from heaven? Seeing that there is no one who can contradict these things, you ought to be quiet and do nothing rashly. These men whom you have brought here have been doing no harm. If Demetrius and the others who are with him have any quarrel with any man, let them go to the courts about it and not make a riot here. We are in danger of being put in prison for this uproar, because there is no good reason for it."

When he had said this, he dismissed the crowd.

After the crowd of people had gone home and the city was quiet again, Paul called the disciples together to say goodbye to them. There were many Christians, for he had been there for three years. And so once more Paul set out on his journey.

CHAPTER 79

The Young Man Who Fell Asleep

ACTS 20

From Ephesus, Paul went to Macedonia and then to Greece. He visited all the places where he had been before, where churches had been started. He did not stay long in any place, for he was very eager to be in Jerusalem on the day of Pentecost.

Finally he came to the city of Troas, on the seashore. There he stayed for a week, preaching and teaching. When Sunday came, all the Christian people of the city met in a large room on the third floor of a building to hear Paul preach. They were very eager to hear him, for the only way they could learn more about Jesus was by hearing Paul or another apostle preach. The New Testament had not yet been written. The new Christians could not go home and take down their Bibles and read over the things which they had forgotten. They just had to try hard to remember what Paul said to them.

Paul had much to say, for he would never again be able to come to preach to the church of Troas. He kept on with his preaching until midnight, and the people listened to every word.

Since the room was crowded, one young man had perched himself on a window sill to listen. Near the end of the long sermon the young man fell asleep. Before anyone could catch him, he tumbled backward out of the third-story window and fell all the way to the ground.

Paul ran down the stairs as fast as he could, but the young man was dead when he reached him. Paul threw himself upon the young man's body and held him tight. He said to the people, "Don't cry, for he is alive again." At first they could hardly believe, but then they saw that it was true. God had given Paul power to bring the dead to life.

The people went upstairs again. They had communion together, eating bread and drinking wine in remembrance of the broken body and shed blood of the Lord Jesus, as he had commanded his followers to do.

Paul stayed and talked all night long, until daylight came. Then at last he said goodbye and went down to the ship which was to take him away. In it he sailed around the coast of Asia. He did not have time to stop at all the places he had visited on his first trip.

At about this time Paul was joined by a man who stayed with him on all the rest of his journeys. He was a doctor, and a very good man. His name was Luke.

It was now thirty years since Jesus had gone up to heaven. His disciples had been preaching all that time and there were now many Christian churches, far and wide, with thousands of members.

So far nothing had been written about Jesus. But now the apostles saw that they must write down all that they knew about him. Otherwise, after they were dead there would be no one who knew it all as it happened.

Matthew wrote an account of the life of Jesus, which is now the first book in our New Testament. Mark, who was not one of the twelve apostles, but a disciple, did the same. Dr. Luke wrote another. Like Mark, he was not one of the twelve apostles, but he had followed Jesus and he knew about the life of Jesus from the beginning. Besides writing this story of the life of Jesus, Dr. Luke wrote an account of what the apostles did after Christ's death. He could do this very well, because he travelled with Paul for many years. This book of Luke is called "The Acts of the Apostles."

A long time after these first three books were written, John, the beloved disciple, wrote another account of the life of Christ.

And Paul wrote letters to the churches he loved so dearly. In a letter to the Ephesians he wrote this to the children: "Children, obey your parents in the Lord, for this is right." The Christians at Ephesus read Paul's letter in church on Sundays, just as we sometimes do. It is God's Word, for God told Paul what to write.

There was a splendid temple of Diana at Ephesus. Acts 19

Day after day the tempest raged. Acts 27

God helped every one of these men to write. He told them exactly what to say, because He wanted these books to be part of the Bible, without any mistakes at all in them. God's telling the writers what to say we call "inspiration."

The whole Bible is God's book, although it was written by many different men, at different times. Everything in it was put there by Him.

CHAPTER 80

Back to Jerusalem

ACTS 20, 21

As Paul and his friends sailed around the coast of Asia, they came near the city of Ephesus, where Paul had preached for a long time, and where he had founded a church.

Since Paul was in a hurry to get to Jerusalem in time for the Day of Pentecost, he could not stop at Ephesus. Still he wanted to see his friends, the members of the church. So he sent word to them to come to the seashore to meet him.

When they came, he said to them, "I am going up to Jerusalem, and I do not know what is going to happen to me there. Everywhere I go, the Holy Spirit tells me that I shall have trouble in Jerusalem, that I shall be arrested and shall suffer. But I will not stop on that account, not even for fear of losing my life. It is my joy to preach the gospel of the grace of God. Now I know that you will never see me again. But do not forget that for three years I taught you. And God will take care of you."

When Paul had spoken these words, he kneeled down on the seashore and prayed with them. They all wept, sorrowing most of all because he had said that they would see his face no more. They walked with him to the ship, and after the last sorrowful goodbyes, Paul sailed away.

The ship sailed around the coast of Asia, stopping at many places. At last it reached Caesarea. In this city there lived a man of whom you have heard before—Philip, who talked to the black man from Africa on the road through the desert.

Philip was the minister of the church in Caesarea. He had four daughters who were a great help to him, for they all were prophets to whom God spoke.

While Paul was staying at Philip's house, a prophet came there. Taking Paul's girdle, he tied his own hands and feet and said, "The Holy Spirit told me that the Jews at Jerusalem would bind the hands and feet of the man who owns this girdle."

Luke writes in his book, "When we heard that, we begged Paul not to go up to Jerusalem, but he answered, 'What do you mean by weeping and breaking my heart? For I am ready not only to be bound, but also to die at Jerusalem for the Lord Jesus.' So when he would not be persuaded, we stopped and said, 'The Lord's will be done.'"

Paul had to travel only a little way to go to Jerusalem. The Christians there were very glad to see him. "The next day," says Luke, "we went to see James." This James was the brother of Jesus. He had been made the bishop of the church at Jerusalem. All the elders of the church of Jerusalem gathered at his house on the day Paul arrived in order to greet him. For a long time they had not had news of the missionary journey. Paul had not been able to write letters to the church at Jerusalem to tell them how he was getting along, and they had had to wait for news until his return.

Paul told them all the things that God had done by him among the heathen in Asia—how he had preached and founded churches in Antioch, and Iconium, and Lystra, and Philippi, and Athens, and Corinth, and Ephesus, and Troas. He told them how he had been stoned at Lystra and put in prison at Philippi, and how much trouble he had had in Ephesus because of the image of the heathen goddess Diana, and how God had delivered him out of all his troubles.

When James and the others heard how many heathen had turned to the Lord through Paul's preaching they glorified and thanked the Lord.

CHAPTER 81

An Uproar in the Temple

ACTS 21

After Paul had been in Jerusalem for about a week, he went into the Temple one day. Some of the Jews saw him there. They knew that Paul had been walking around Jerusalem with some friends from Asia, and they thought he had brought them into the Temple with him. Paul had not done so. All Jews knew that no foreigners were allowed inside God's house.

But Paul's enemies thought that they had caught him in a crime. They called out, "Men of Israel, help! This is the man who has been teaching men everywhere against the law of Moses and against our Temple. He has brought Greeks into our Temple and made the holy place unclean!"

When the people heard this, they ran to the spot quickly and pulled Paul out of the Temple. Then they shut the doors so that no more Greeks could enter the building. For they believed that Paul had really taken his friends into the Temple with him. They were so angry at the thought that they wanted to kill him. A mob gathered together, screaming, "Kill him! Kill him!"

Somebody quickly ran to tell the chief captain of the Roman soldiers that a great mob was gathering, and that all Jerusalem was in an uproar.

It was the chief captain's business to keep order in Jerusalem. As soon as he heard that the whole city was upset and that the crowd was going to kill somebody, he took several hundred soldiers and went just as fast as he could to the place where the disturbance was.

While the soldiers were still a short distance away, the Jews saw them coming and stopped beating Paul. The first thing the captain did was to put two chains on Paul so that he could not escape. Then he turned to the wild mob and said, "Who is this man, and what has he done?"

Some yelled one thing and some another. They all shouted together, making such a noise and confusion that the chief captain could not understand a word they said. At last he commanded his soldiers to take Paul inside the castle.

The Jews pushed and shoved roughly and violently, screaming, "Away with him! Away with him!" The soldiers could not get Paul up the stairs through the crowd. At last they actually had to lift him up on their shoulders and carry him up.

As they were taking him into the castle, Paul said in Greek to the chief captain, "May I speak to you?"

Astonished to hear Paul speak in Greek, the chief captain said to him, "Can you speak Greek? Are you not that Egyptian who some time ago led four thousand murderers into the wilderness?"

Paul answered, "No, I am not an Egyptian. I am a Jew, and I beg you to let me speak to the people."

So Paul stood at the top of the stairs. All around him were the soldiers with their spears, to protect him from the crowd. He beckoned with his hand to the people to keep quiet so that he could talk.

Paul started to speak in Hebrew. When they heard that it was their own language that he used, they quieted down finally.

CHAPTER 82

Paul's Speech to the Jews

ACTS 22

Paul looked over the crowd of angry Jews who had pulled him out of the Temple, yelling, "Kill him!" Now they were listening to hear what he would say.

Paul began very politely. "Men, brethren, and fathers: I am a Jew. I was born in Tarsus, but I went to school here, in the city of

Jerusalem. The great Gamaliel was my teacher. I was very earnest about all the Jewish laws, just as you are. I hated the Christians just as you do. I hunted them down, and had them arrested and put into prison. I even persecuted them to death.

"The high priest knows these things. He gave me letters to the priests in Damascus, so that I could arrest any Christians in Damascus, and could bring them here to be punished.

"But something wonderful happened to me on the way to Damascus. When I had almost reached the city, about noon, suddenly a great light from Heaven shone round about me. I was so startled and frightened that I fell to the ground. I heard a voice saying unto me, 'Saul, Saul, why do you persecute me?'

"I answered the voice and said, 'Who are you, Lord?' He answered, 'I am Jesus of Nazareth. You are persecuting me.'

"Those who were with me saw the light, but they did not hear the voice. I said, 'What shall I do, Lord?'

"And the Lord said to me, 'Arise and go into Damascus. There it shall be told you what you shall do.'

"But I could not see because of the glory of the light. It had blinded me, and those who were with me had to lead me by the hand. So I came into Damascus, and after I had been there three days, a good man came to see me. He said, 'Brother Saul, receive your sight.' So my blindness went away, and I saw him.

"This man said to me, 'You are not to fight against the Christians any more, for they are God's people. God wants you to become a Christian, for He has chosen you to see Jesus and to hear his voice. You shall go into all the world and tell about Jesus. Now rise and be baptized and wash away your sins.

"After this, I came to Jerusalem. While I was praying here in the Temple, the Lord said to me, 'Make haste and leave Jerusalem, for the people will not listen to you here. I will send you far away to the heathen.'"

The crowd listened quietly until Paul spoke about the heathen. Then they became angry, for they did not believe that God wished to save anybody except the Jews. They thought that only the Jews were

God's people. They did not remember that God had said, "All the earth is Mine."

So when Paul said that God sent him to the heathen, they began to yell, "Away with him! Away with him! Away with such a fellow from the earth, for it is not fit that he should live."

When the chief captain saw this, he commanded the soldiers to bring Paul into the castle and give him a beating, in order to find out why the people were so furious against him.

The soldiers led Paul into the castle and began to bind his hands and feet with strips of leather. But Paul asked them, "Is it lawful to beat a man who is a Roman?"

When the soldier in charge heard this, he hurried to the chief captain and said to him, "Be careful what you do, for this man is a Roman."

This was disturbing news, for it was against the law to beat a Roman citizen without his first having been tried and found guilty of some crime. The chief captain went at once to Paul. "Tell me," he said, "is it true that you are a Roman?"

Paul replied, "Yes."

"I am too," answered the captain. "But I had to pay a great sum of money to become a Roman citizen."

Paul said, "I was born a Roman citizen, for I was born in a Roman city."

Hearing this, the captain took off the chains that bound Paul. He was afraid that he would be punished for putting chains on a man who was a Roman citizen.

CHAPTER 83

A Wicked Oath

Acts 23

In Paul's day only Roman citizens had a right to be tried and to defend themselves when anyone accused them of doing wrong. Other people were beaten, to make them confess. When a Roman was tried, the man who accused him of doing wrong had to come and tell his complaint. Then the prisoner had a chance to defend himself.

Since Paul was a Roman the captain commanded the chief priests, who said Paul should not be allowed to live, to come to the judgment hall and tell what they had against him.

When Paul entered the hall in which he was to be tried, he looked at the crowd of people. At once he saw that part of them were Pharisees and part were Sadducees. The Pharisees believed the Old Testament and tried to follow its teachings, but the Sadducees did not. They did not believe that God takes interest in people or that He helps them. They did not believe that people live again after they have died, or that there are any angels in heaven. On account of these things the two groups hated each other bitterly.

Paul knew this. When he saw that these enemies had come here together to accuse him, he called out, "Men and brethren, I am a Pharisee, and the son of a Pharisee, and my being here has to do with the resurrection of the dead."

As soon as he said this a fight arose among the Jews. The Pharisees took Paul's part. "Why, this man is all right," they said. "What if an angel or a spirit really did speak to him on the way to Damascus? We do not wish to fight against God."

The Pharisees believed that angels and spirits come to earth and speak to men. The Sadducees did not believe that there are any such things as angels or spirits.   In a few minutes there was a fight among the Sadducees and Pharisees.

The Pharisees tried to get hold of Paul, and they shouted, "This man has done nothing wrong.   He says an angel has spoken to him." At the same time the Sadducees, trying to get Paul away from the Pharisees, yelled, "There are no such things as angels."   Between them there was such shouting and fighting that the captain was afraid Paul would be pulled to pieces.   Finally he commanded the soldiers to go down and take Paul away from them by force, and bring him into the castle.

That night the Lord came and stood by Paul and comforted him, saying, "Do not be afraid, Paul, for I will not let the people of Jerusalem kill you.   I am going to send you to Rome to preach about me there."

These words were a great comfort to Paul. Now he knew that, no matter what might happen to him, the Lord would save him out of the hands of the Jews.

Many of the Jews were furious because Paul was out of their reach.   More than forty of them banded together and swore that they would not eat nor drink until they had killed him.   Then they went to the chief priests and elders and said, "We have bound ourselves under a great curse that we will neither eat nor drink until we have killed Paul."

What do you think would happen today if a band of men should come to the governor and tell him such a thing? They would be thrown into prison before they knew what was happening to them.   They would be tried for attempting murder.

That is what would have happened to the forty men who wanted to kill Paul if the priests had been good men.   But instead of arresting them, the priests made a bargain with them.   They were glad to find some men who would kill Paul for them.

The forty Jews said to the chief priests and elders, "Tell the chief captain tomorrow that you have some questions that you want to ask Paul.   Persuade him to bring Paul out to you.   We will lie in wait for him and kill him on the way."

CHAPTER 84

How Paul Was Saved

ACTS 23

God was taking care of Paul. He was not going to let the Jews kill him, as they planned. A son of Paul's sister heard the wicked plan of the forty Jews. He went right into the castle and told his uncle Paul.

When he heard the news, Paul called one of the guards and said to him, "Bring this young man to the chief captain, for he has something to tell him."

The soldier led the young man to the captain and said, "Paul, the prisoner, called me and told me to bring this young man to you, because he has something to say to you." Then the guard went away, leaving them alone.

The young man said, "The chief priests and elders have agreed with some rough men that tomorrow they will ask you to let Paul come down into the council, as if they wanted to ask him some questions. The rough men will be waiting, and just as soon as he comes down they will be ready to kill him. When they ask you, O captain, to let Paul go, do not do so; for there are more than forty of them, and they have bound themselves with an oath they will neither eat nor drink until they have killed him."

When he had finished, the captain answered, "You have done right to come and tell me. I will take care of Paul. You keep still about what you have told me. Don't say a word to anyone." Then he let the young man go.

At once the captain began to arrange to take care of Paul. He called to him two centurions, captains over a hundred soldiers. "Make ready two hundred soldiers to go to Caesarea at two o'clock tonight," he ordered. "Take two hundred spearmen also, and seventy horsemen. Bring Paul safely to Felix, the governor, at Caesarea. Take animals for everyone to ride on so that you can hurry."

Caesarea was the city where the governor always lived, and it was full of soldiers. Wicked Herod, who was once the governor of the land, had had his palace there. He was dead now, and Felix was governor in his place. Felix was a much better man than Herod had been.

To Felix the captain wrote this letter:

"This man, Paul, was caught by the Jews. They were getting ready to kill him, but I heard that he was a Roman, and so I came with an army, and rescued him.

"When I asked the Jews what he had done, they said he had broken some of their Jewish laws, but I found he had done nothing worthy of death or of being put in prison.

"Hearing that the Jews were planning to kill him, I have sent him to you. I have also told the Jews to come and tell you, if they have any fault to find with him."

The two centurions took the letter and called their soldiers together. At two o'clock that night they were all ready. Off they started, all four hundred seventy of them, riding on horses or donkeys, and riding as fast as they could go.

When the morning light came, they were a long way from Jerusalem and it was safe to let the soldiers go back. Only the seventy horsemen went the rest of the way with Paul.

At last they reached Caesarea and gave the letter to Felix. The governor read the letter. Then he said to Paul. "I will hear your defense when the priests and elders come to accuse you."

CHAPTER 85

The Trial

ACTS 24

Five days after Paul reached the governor's city safely, Ananias and the elders came to accuse him before the court. Governor Felix called a meeting and brought Paul out, to find what he had done to turn the Jews against him.

The Jews had brought with them a man who was a fine public speaker. He began by addressing the governor, Felix, most politely:

"Most noble Felix, we are very thankful to you that you are such a good governor, and that you have done so many good deeds to our nation. — But we do not want to tire you with speaking, and so we beg that you will listen to only a few words.

"This man here is an annoying fellow. He stirs up trouble wherever he goes. Besides, he is a ringleader of the Nazarenes, or Christians. He has mocked our holy Temple. We were going to punish him for that, but the captain came with his soldiers, and took him by force out of our hands. If you examine Paul you will find these things are true."

All the Jews nodded their heads and said, "Yes, all this is true."

Then the governor beckoned to Paul that it was his turn to speak. Paul was glad to be able to defend himself before Felix. This man had a Jewish wife, and he knew much about the Jews and their religion that the Romans did not understand.

Paul began: "I am glad to speak for myself, for I know that you have been a judge to this nation for many years. It is not true that I was making trouble in the city, and they can not prove what they say. But it is true that I am a follower of Jesus and that I believe all the law and the prophets. The only fault that they can find in me is that I cried out to them, 'I believe in the resurrection of the dead.'"

Hearing Paul speak, Felix was sure that he had done nothing wrong. Felix had heard many things about the Nazarenes, as the Christians were called by the Jews; and he wished to learn more about them from Paul. The high priests and elders were sent home, so that Felix might talk to the captain of the soldiers in Jerusalem before deciding what to do. Paul was kept in Caesarea with a soldier to guard him. The soldier was ordered to let Paul do as he liked, and to let all his friends come to see him.

It was very pleasant for Paul, there in Caesarea. Even though he was a prisoner, he had a great deal of liberty. Many of his friends in the city came to see him, for there was a large Christian church there, which Paul had visited on his way to Jerusalem.

A few days after the Jews had returned to Jerusalem, Felix and his wife Drusilla, who was a Jew, sent for Paul. They wished to hear more about Jesus and the new group called "Christians."

Paul talked very earnestly about Jesus to Felix and his wife. The governor was very much interested. But when Paul spoke about the great judgment day that is coming, Felix trembled in terror. At last he said to Paul, "That is enough for this time. When it is convenient I will be glad to hear more, and I will call for you again."

Felix often sent for Paul, for he was very much interested in what Paul said. But he did not become a Christian, and he did not let Paul go. The reason he kept him was this: he hoped that Paul would pay him for freedom. But Paul did not, and after two years another man, called Festus, came to be governor.

Instead of letting Paul go free before the new governor came, Felix kept him a prisoner, because he knew this would please the Jews. Paul had been a prisoner now for more than two years, but he had not been idle. He was permitted to see his friends, and probably Philip often asked him to preach in the Christian church. In many ways Paul managed to tell people of Jesus, even though he was no longer able to "go into all the world."

CHAPTER 86

The Appeal to Caesar

ACTS 25

When Festus became governor, Paul was still a prisoner. After three days in his palace at Caesarea, the new governor went down to Jerusalem.

The high priest and the elders had not forgotten about Paul, though two years had passed since those forty men vowed not to eat or drink till they had killed him. Surely, that vow had been broken long ago, for they could not live without eating and drinking.

Now that the new governor Festus had come, they again tried to get rid of Paul. They asked Festus to send for him to come down to Jerusalem for trial. Their plan was to hide on the road and kill Paul.

Perhaps the old governor, Felix, had warned Festus not to let this prisoner go down to Jerusalem, for Festus would not listen. He said that he was going to keep Paul at Caesarea. If any of the Jews had fault to find with Paul, they could travel to Caesarea and accuse him there.

When Festus went back to Caesarea, about ten days later, some of the Jews went with him to accuse Paul.

The next day Festus sat on the judgment seat and commanded that Paul be brought. The Jews at once began to find fault with Paul, accusing him of many things which he had never done. None of the things which they said could be proved.

Then it was Paul's turn to speak. He said, "I have not done anything wrong against the law of the Jews, nor against the Temple, nor against the Roman emperor, Caesar."

Festus wanted to please the Jews if he could, for he had just come to rule over them. He said, "Will you go up to Jerusalem to be judged of these things?"

Paul knew that if he should go to Jerusalem, the Jews would lie in wait along the road to kill him. He knew that he would never reach Jerusalem alive. He also knew that as a Roman citizen he had certain rights. If he did not think that his country-men were giving him a fair trial, he could demand to be tried by the highest ruler of all, the emperor Caesar in Rome.

So when Festus asked him if he would go up to Jerusalem to be tried there, Paul said, "I stand at Caesar's judgment seat. I have done nothing wrong to the Jews, as you very well know. They cannot prove any of these things of which they accuse me. I appeal to Caesar."

Now that Paul had appealed to Caesar, Festus was obliged to send him to Rome, whether he wanted to or not. So he answered, "Since you have appealed to Caesar, unto Caesar you shall go."

A few days later, the king Agrippa and his wife Bernice made a visit to Caesarea to greet the new governor, Festus.

Agrippa was the ruler of the land east of the Jordan River, sent out to rule the Jews for the Roman emperor, as Festus had been. Festus, who had recently come to the land, wanted to be friends with Agrippa.

One day he said, "King Agrippa, there is a man here who was left a prisoner by Felix. When I went down to Jerusalem, the Jews there told me that they wanted to have him killed. I answered that it is not the custom of the Romans to condemn anyone until he has a chance to speak for himself.

"So when the Jews came here to Caesarea, I sat on the judgment seat and commanded the man to be brought. When the Jews came to accuse him they did not have anything important to say. They accused him only of some offense against their own religion and about somebody named Jesus, who was dead, though Paul said he was alive. I did not think that such questions were very important, and I asked Paul if he would go down to Jerusalem to be judged. But Paul appealed to Caesar, and so to Caesar he shall be sent."

Agrippa said, "I should like to hear this man myself."

"Very well," said Festus. "You shall hear him tomorrow."

CHAPTER 87

A King is Almost Persuaded

ACTS 26

In the judgment hall of the Roman governor all the important people of Caesarea were gathered together. Some of them had come because they wanted to see King Agrippa, who was visiting the governor. Others wanted to hear the prisoner Paul defend himself before Agrippa and Festus. Perhaps Philip and some of the other Christians were there too, to listen to Paul. King Agrippa and his wife Bernice put on their finest clothes and came to the judgment hall with much pomp, as we go to hear a lecturer. They knew that Paul was a learned man and a fine speaker.

Paul was brought in, a prisoner. Then governor Festus stood up before the people. Turning first to King Agrippa and then to the crowd he said,

"King Agrippa and all men here present, you see this man, Paul, who the Jews say ought not to live any longer. But I found that he has done nothing worthy of death, and he himself has appealed to Caesar. So I decided to send him to Rome. But I do not like to send him to the emperor when I have no definite complaint to make against him. It seems to me unreasonable to send a prisoner and not to write the crimes laid against him. I have brought him out for you to hear, King Agrippa, so that perhaps when you have heard him, you can tell me what to write to the emperor Caesar."

As Festus sat down King Agrippa said to Paul, "You may speak for yourself."

King Agrippa was different from the other people before whom Paul had spoken. He really understood Jewish customs and religion. The other rulers had not been able to understand either the charges of the Jews nor Paul's defense.

Paul began, "I think myself happy, King Agrippa, that I am to speak before you, because I know that you understand all the customs of the Jews. So I beg that you will hear me patiently.

"All the Jews know what kind of man I have been all my life. They know that I was a Pharisee, and that I lived an earnest life. It is because I believe that Jesus Christ is the one so long promised to our fathers that they find fault with me. But why should it seem strange if God raises the dead?

"I used to think that those who believed in Jesus of Nazareth were wrong, and I did many things against the Christians. I shut up many of them in prison, and when they were put to death, I voted against them. I punished them, and I was so furious against them that I even followed them to strange cities. I went to Damascus with letters from the high priest, to arrest all the Christians whom I could find there.

"As I was travelling to Damascus, about midday, O king, I saw a light from Heaven, brighter than the sun, shining round about me and those with me. When we had all fallen to the earth, I heard a voice speaking to me in the Hebrew language, 'Saul, Saul, why do you persecute me? It is hard for you to kick against the pricks.'

"And I said, 'Who are you, Lord?'

"He said, 'I am Jesus, whom you are persecuting. I have appeared to you to make you one of my ministers. I will send you to the heathen, to open their eyes, and to turn them from darkness to light, and from the power of Satan to God, so that they may have their sins forgiven, and may go to Heaven, with all others who believe on me!'

"O King Agrippa, I obeyed this heavenly vision, and I did what Jesus told me to do. I preached, first in Damascus and then in Jerusalem and then to the heathen. That is the reason why the Jews caught me in the Temple and tried to kill me. But God has kept me from being hurt, and I still go on preaching just what Moses and the prophets prophesied, — that Christ should suffer and that he should rise from the dead."

When Paul had finished, the new governor, Festus, cried with a loud voice, "Paul, you are mad. You have studied so much that it has turned your head."

Paul replied, "I am not mad, most noble Festus. I am speaking truth and soberness. For King Agrippa knows all about these things that I have been saying. I am sure that he knows, for none of these things were done in a corner secretly."

Turning to Agrippa, Paul said, "King Agrippa, do you believe the prophets? I know that you believe them."

"Paul, you have almost persuaded me to be a Christian," answered the king.

Paul said, "I would to God that not only you, but all those who hear me today, were Christians, as I am myself, but not in chains."

The king arose to leave the hall, and the audience followed him. The king and Festus went by themselves and said, "This man has done nothing worthy of death or of chains." And Agrippa said to Festus, "This man might have been set at liberty if he had not appealed to Caesar."

CHAPTER 88

Paul Sets Out for Rome

ACTS 27

Since Paul had appealed to Caesar, it was decided that he should be sent to Rome. Doctor Luke went with him, and wrote all about the journey, which was a very exciting one.

Before they started out, Paul and some other prisoners were given into the charge of a Roman centurion named Julius. The prisoners were going to be well guarded on their trip, for the centurion had one hundred soldiers under him.

Luke wrote, "We entered into a sail boat. The next day we stopped at Sidon. Julius, the centurion, was very kind to Paul and let him go on shore at Sidon to see his friends and eat with them. Then we got into the ship again and sailed near the island of Cyprus. It was hard sailing, for the wind blew the wrong way."

This was long before there were any steamboats. There were only rowboats and sailing vessels. When the wind blew from the wrong direction, or when it blew too hard, sailors had a difficult and dangerous time guiding a sail boat.

Besides, the sailors had no compasses, as we have, which point to the north all the time. When they were out of sight of land, the only way they could tell which way they were going was by the sun in the day time, or by the stars at night. When it was cloudy or stormy, and they could not see the sun or the stars, they could not tell which way they were going.

Dr. Luke wrote, "We had to sail very slowly for many days, because the wind blew from the wrong direction. We could hardly move against it. But at last we came to the island of Crete, and we stopped at a place called 'Fair Havens.'

"We waited there for better weather, so that we could sail more safely. For many days we waited, but the weather kept getting worse instead of better. At last Paul said, 'Sirs, I am sure that if we try to go on with our voyage at this time of year, we will have great misfortunes. Our ship will be destroyed, and the goods that the ship is loaded with will be injured, and we will be in great danger of losing our lives. We had better stay here till the winter is over and good weather comes.'

"But the centurion, the captain of the soldiers, listened to the owner of the ship rather than to Paul. They talked of trying to go a little farther, to a town called Phenice, which was on the other side of the island.

"Fair Havens, the place to which the ship had come, was not very comfortable for spending the winter. Most of them said it would be better to try to get to Phenice. After a few days the stormy weather passed away, the bright sunshine came out, and the south wind blew softly. They thought it would be safe to leave Fair Havens and to try to get to Phenice.

"When we had left the harbor and sailed along the coast of the island, a terrible wind sprang up. It was a real hurricane.

"We were too far from the island of Crete to turn back now. The wind was so terrible that we could not manage the ship at all. We could only let her go where she was driven.

"The sky turned black as night. The rain poured down in sheets. The lightning streaked across the sky. The hurricane howled and shrieked and the waves ran mountain high.

"Our ship was tossed to and fro like an egg shell. We were lifted to the crest of a mounting wave, only to be dropped in the trough of the next one. We did everything that we could to make the ship lighter. We threw overboard everything that we could lay hands on. We helped the sailors pull down the sails and the masts and all the tackling of the ship and toss it into the sea.

"Day after day, the storm kept on. Day after day the tempest raged. No sun nor stars appeared in the sky. At last we gave up all hope.

"Then Paul stood up among us and said, 'Sirs, you should have listened to me, and not have sailed away from Crete. But do not give up hope, for none of you will die, but only the ship will be lost. For this night the angel of my God stood by me and said to me, "Do not be afraid, Paul, for God will save you, so that you can go to Rome to see Caesar. And God will save all those who sail with you, for your sake." So be of good cheer, for what God says is true, and we shall all be saved, but we must first be cast on an island.' "

CHAPTER 89

The Shipwreck

Acts 27

Let us go on with Luke's story of Paul's journey to Rome:

"We had now been sailing in a terrible storm for two weeks. One night, as the wind was driving us about in the sea, the sailors thought that we were drawing near to land. They dropped a line into the sea to measure the depth of the water, and found that it was only twenty fathoms deep. Soon they dropped another line into the sea and this time it was only fifteen fathoms deep.

"Then we knew that we were near to some land. There was danger that we would strike rocks near the shore and be dashed to pieces. So we cast four anchors out into the sea to keep the ship from crashing on the rocks.

"It was a dark night, and the waves were high. We could see no land, but we knew that it must be near because the water was not deep. We longed for the light of day to come.

"The sailors tried to save themselves by letting a little boat down into the sea. They were going to row to shore, leaving us to perish with the ship. They hoped that in the darkness of the night the master of the ship would not see them.

"But Paul saw them letting the boat down, and he said to the centurion, 'If the sailors leave the ship, you will be drowned.' So the captain would not let the sailors go. The soldiers cut away the ropes and let the boat drop down into the sea and drift away.

"In the dawning of the day Paul said to all the men in the ship, 'I beg of you to eat some food, for it is now fourteen days since you have tasted anything. It will be far better for you to eat. Not a hair shall fall from the head of any of you.'

"With these words Paul took some bread. Looking up to heaven, he gave thanks to God and ate it. When the men saw Paul so cheerful, they were encouraged and they too ate some food.

"Counting all of us in the ship, there were two hundred and seventy-six men. When everyone had eaten as much as he wanted, the sailors tried to make the ship lighter, so that it would float in shallow water. They threw into the sea the wheat with which the ship was loaded.

"When the daylight came, we saw a strange new land. Close to us there was a little bay with a smooth beach. We decided to try to drive the ship into the little bay, which seemed to be a safe place to land.

"'First of all, the sailors loosened the boat from the four anchors that they had let down to keep the ship from moving. Then they raised the main sail to the wind and headed the ship towards the shore. They found a place where the waters ran in toward the shore, and they let the waves carry the ship with all their force.

"Soon the ship ran aground. The front part stuck fast in the sand and could not be moved, but the back was broken up by the violent pounding of the wild waves.

"The soldiers advised the centurion to kill all the prisoners, for fear that they would swim away and escape. The centurion, however, knew that Paul was a good and innocent man, and that it would not be right to kill him. So he commanded all who could swim to cast themselves into the sea and swim ashore.

"The waves were pounding on the ship. Those who could not swim were afraid to stay on her, and they were still more afraid to jump into the raging sea. But the ship was breaking so fast that at last they found courage to cast themselves overboard, some on boards and some on broken pieces of the ship.

"Every one of them reached the land safely."

CHAPTER 90

The Rescue

ACTS 28

After telling about the shipwreck on Paul's journey to Rome, Luke writes:

"When we were all safe ashore on the island, we looked around. We soon knew that we were on the island of Melita.

"The people there were very kind to us. They built a big fire to warm us. We were soaking wet, and almost frozen from being in the sea so long. It was still raining, and very cold.

"As Paul gathered a bundle of sticks to burn in the fire, a poisonous viper came out from among them and fastened on his hand. The heathen people saw the deadly snake on Paul's hand and they whispered among themselves, 'This man must be a murderer. He has escaped drowning in the sea, but he is now going to be punished for the sin he has done, for that snake will surely kill him.'

"But Paul shook off the viper into the fire and felt no harm. They watched him closely for a long time, waiting to see his hand swell, expecting him to fall down dead. For a long time they waited. When nothing happened to him, they changed their minds, and said that he must be a god come down to earth in the shape of a man.

"The chief man of the island was named Publius. His house was near the place where we were cast on shore. He took care of us for three days, very kindly.

"This man had a poor old father who was very sick. Paul went in to see the old man. Laying his hands upon him, he prayed, and the man was made well.

"When the others on the island found that Paul could heal the sick, they brought others to be healed. All who came were cured.

"We stayed on the island for three months, till the winter was past. The people honored us very highly. When we left, they gave us freely all that we needed.

"At last we found another ship, whose name was *The Twin Brothers*. She was going from Egypt to Rome, but she had stayed all winter in the island to wait for good weather.

"When she sailed, we sailed in her. Landing at Syracuse in Sicily, we stayed there three days. When the south wind blew, we boarded the ship again and came to a city on the coast of Italy. There we found that we had friends. We left the ship and stayed with them seven days. After a week there, we went towards Rome, going by land.

"The Christians of Rome heard of us and came to meet us at the Market of Appius and the Three Taverns. Oh, how glad Paul was to see them! He thanked God, and felt braver.

"At last we came to Rome, and our long journey was ended. The centurion sent the prisoners to the captain of the guard in Rome. Paul was not sent to prison. He was allowed to rent a house and to live there by himself, with only one soldier staying with him as a guard. He was free to go wherever he wished, and to have his friends visit him. But wherever he went he had to wear a chain which was very heavy and uncomfortable.

"After he had been in Rome for three days, Paul sent for the leaders of the Jews there. They had not heard of the trouble in Jerusalem, but they were glad to talk to Paul, for they had heard many things about the Christians. And so Paul talked with them for a long time about Jesus, the promised Savior. Some of the Jews believed him, but others would not listen.

"Paul lived in Rome for two years before the emperor was ready to hear him, preaching to everyone."

CHAPTER 91

The Hero of Faith

II CORINTHIANS 11, 12

After Paul and Luke reached Rome, their story ends. We know nothing more about Paul, except that he died bravely as a soldier of Jesus.

In all the years since that time there has been no greater preacher and missionary than Paul. He spent his life telling people about Jesus. He founded churches all over Asia Minor and Greece. Once he talked about going to Spain, but we do not know whether he ever went.

Paul wrote many letters to the churches he had founded, explaining about Jesus. We can read some of these letters too, because they became parts of the New Testament. The Spirit of God helped him, telling him what to write. Like the rest of the Bible, Paul's letters are God's words.

Paul was a great hero. He endured great suffering for his beloved master. Five times he was cruelly beaten. Each time he was given the worst beating allowed by the law of the Jews. Three times he was beaten with rods. Once he was stoned and left for dead. Three times he was shipwrecked, and once he was in the water a whole day and a night. Just think of being on the sea for so long a time, kept afloat only by some piece of a ship or some boards! Often the men to whom Paul preached became so angry that they acted like wild beasts who wanted to tear him apart.

But many beautiful, wonderful things happened to Paul, too, which strengthened him for his work. Jesus spoke to him right out of heaven, as Paul was going to Damascus. Many times God spoke to him, bringing comfort and hope.

Once Paul was taken right up to Heaven. It was all so wonderful that he could never tell if he was really taken to Heaven, or whether he only saw it in a vision. But he knew that he had seen the glories of Heaven and had heard words so wonderful that no man could ever speak them.

Although Paul was glad to work and fight for Jesus in this world, he often longed to go to Heaven to be with Jesus, for he said that was far better. Near the end of his life he said, "I have fought the good fight, I have finished the course, I have kept the faith. Henceforth, there is laid up for me a crown of righteousness, which the Lord, the righteous Judge, shall give to me at that day." Soon afterward, this splendid soldier of the cross was killed in Rome.

It is thought that Peter also died in Rome at about the same time, killed by the wicked emperor Nero. There is a legend that when Peter was about to die, he asked that he might be crucified with his head at the bottom of the cross. This was the most painful way to die, but Peter felt that he was not worthy to die in the same way that his beloved Lord had died.

Like Paul, Peter wrote some of the books of the New Testament. You will find them in your Bible under the names "I Peter" and "II Peter."

Luke wrote "The Gospel according to Luke," and "The Acts of the Apostles."

Matthew wrote a story of the life of Jesus, and Mark wrote another.

James, the Lord's brother, wrote the book called "James."

Judas, the son of Alpheus, wrote one letter called "Jude."

John, the beloved disciple, wrote about the life of Jesus, and he also wrote three little letters, the First, Second and Third Epistles of John.

John was the youngest of the twelve apostles, and the one who lived the longest. Toward the end of his life he was arrested. Instead of being sent to prison, he was sent to a lonely little island, called Patmos. While John was on this island, he wrote the last book of the Bible, called "The Revelation of St. John." It tells about the things that will happen at the end of the world, and about Heaven.

No one knows who wrote the book of "Hebrews." Some think that Paul wrote it, and some think Apollos did, for the Bible says that he was "an eloquent man, and mighty in the scriptures."

All these writers were inspired by God. That is, God told them what to say. The New Testament is His book just as the Old Testament is. Together they form the Bible, which gives us the Word of Life.

CHAPTER 92

The Last Things

I Thessalonians 4, 5; Matthew 25

What happens to us when we die?

When we die, it is only our bodies that die — not our souls. Our souls can not die. They go on living, for ever and ever.

When our bodies die, they are put into coffins and buried in the ground. There they lie until the resurrection day. Since our bodies are made of the same things as the earth, they turn to dust.

When the body dies, the soul leaves the body immediately, without a moment's waiting, and goes to its place.

If we have loved God and have tried to please Him, and have prayed to Him to forgive our sins for Jesus' sake, our soul will go to God's blessed Heaven to live with Jesus.

But if we have not loved God, nor tried to please Him — if we have not prayed to Him to forgive our sins for Jesus' sake, then when we die our soul will not go to Heaven. We will be separated from God and all that is good. We will go to the dreadful place called Hell, where all is wretchedness and misery.

When our bodies lie in the grave, is that the end of them?

No, even when our bodies have turned to dust, they are under God's care and keeping. They will rise again at the resurrection day, when Jesus comes as king.

They will be the very same bodies that we have in this life, but they will then become immortal bodies. This means that they will not die again. They will never decay, nor grow old, nor have pain and weariness and sickness.

Our spirits, which have been living with God in Heaven till the resurrection day, will then join our bodies made glorious.

And after that we shall be forever with the Lord.

And will there be some people still living on this earth, when Jesus comes?

Yes, some people will still be living when Jesus comes. When the trumpet of God sounds forth, Jesus will bring the souls of the dead with him. In a moment, in the twinkling of an eye, the dead bodies shall be raised immortal, and shall clothe the souls which Jesus brought with him. Those who are still alive shall instantly have their mortal bodies changed to immortal ones. In a moment they shall be caught up into the clouds with Jesus, and shall be with the Lord.

When will Jesus come again?

No man knows, not even the angels in Heaven know, when Jesus will come again. But we must all be ready.

For as in the days of Noah, when the people were eating and drinking and not thinking, suddenly the flood came and took them all away; so it shall be when Jesus comes. Therefore we must all watch and be ready, for in an hour when we are not expecting it, the Lord will come.

As the lightning shines from one part of Heaven to the other, so every eye shall see him and every ear shall hear, for the trumpet of God shall sound loud and long, and the Lord will come from Heaven with a shout. He will come in the clouds with power and great glory, and with all his holy angels, and with the voice of the archangel.

The dead in Christ shall rise first, with immortal bodies. Those who still live shall be caught up to meet him in the air. And so they shall be forever with the Lord.

Shall we all see Jesus come again?

Everyone who has ever lived will see Jesus come. Those who are still on the earth will see him coming in the clouds of heaven. Jesus will bring with him the souls of those who have died.

It will be a time of great rejoicing for those who love the Lord. For those who do not, it will be a time of fear and trembling. They will cry to the mountains, "Fall on us!" and to the hills, "Cover us!"

And after the resurrection — what then?

Then will come the judgment day. In the Bible this day is called "That great day of the Lord." On it God shall judge the world. All men and angels and devils must then appear before the throne of Almighty God to be judged.

In that day Jesus will no longer be a humble man, as he was the first time he came to earth. He will be the great Judge of all men and angels and devils. He will sit on the throne of his glory, and everyone who has ever lived shall come and bow down before him.

And he shall separate them one from another, as a shepherd divides the sheep from the goats. For God has kept a book, in which are written all things that we have ever done, good and bad.

In that day the book shall be opened and we shall be judged according to our deeds. Those who have loved Jesus, who have believed on him, and have tried to keep his commandments, will be placed on his right hand. Those who have not loved him or believed on him, who have not tried to keep his commandments, will be placed on his left hand.

Then he will say to those at his right hand, "Come, ye blessed of my father, inherit the kingdom prepared for you from the foundation of the world."

They will have life eternal.

But he will say to those on his left hand, "Depart from me, ye cursed, into everlasting fire, prepared for the devil and his angels."

And these shall go away into everlasting punishment.

CHAPTER 93

The Vision of St. John

REVELATION 1, 5, 21, 22

When the apostle John was an old man, he was sent to the little island of Patmos. He was a prisoner there, a lonely exile. He could not go away again, for the rest of his life.

But while John was there, he had some wonderful visions. He wrote them all down in the Book of Revelation, which became the last book of the Bible. It tells us about Heaven.

John had a vision of Jesus as he looks in Heaven. His head and his hair were as white as snow, and his eyes were like a flame of fire. John fell down, fainting, because he was afraid. But Jesus laid his hand upon John and said to him, "Fear not; I am he that liveth and was dead, and behold I am alive forevermore. Write the things which are going to happen, which you shall see in these visions."

John saw a great white throne, upon which God sat. He saw the dead, small and great, standing before God.

The Book of Life was opened, and the dead were judged according to the things they had done. The sea gave up the dead which were in it, and all men were judged. Whoever was not found in the Book of Life was cast into the lake of fire.

And John saw Jesus looking like a lamb that had been killed. And John heard a new song in Heaven: "Thou art worthy, for thou wast slain, and hast purchased to God with thy blood men of every tribe and tongue and people and nation."

And John heard the voice of many angels round the throne, a great number of them saying loudly, "Worthy is the Lamb that hath been slain, to receive power, and riches, and wisdom, and might, and honor, and glory, and blessing."

And every creature in the Heaven, and on the earth and under the earth and on the sea and all things in them said, "Unto him that sitteth on the throne, and unto the Lamb, be the blessing and the honor, and the glory, and the dominion forever and ever."

In another vision John saw a great multitude, which no man could number, out of every nation and of all tribes and peoples, standing before the throne and before the Lamb, arrayed in white robes, with palms in their hands. And one of the elders said to him, "These are they that came out of the great trial, and they washed their robes and made them white in the blood of the Lamb. Therefore are they before the throne of God, and serve Him day and night in His Temple; and He that sitteth on the throne shall dwell among them. They shall hunger no more, neither thirst any more; neither shall the sun strike upon them, nor any heat. For the Lamb that is in the midst of the throne shall be their shepherd, and shall guide them unto fountains of water of life: and God shall wipe away every tear from their eyes."

Last of all John wrote, "I saw a new heaven and a new earth: for the first heaven and the first earth are passed away . . . And I heard a great voice out of the throne saying, "Behold the tabernacle of God is with men, and He shall dwell with them, and be their God. And God shall wipe away every tear from their eyes; and death shall be no more, neither shall there be mourning, nor crying, nor pain any more.

"And there came to me one of the angels . . . and he carried me away in the spirit to a mountain great and high; and showed me the holy city, Jerusalem, coming down out of Heaven from God.

"And the city was pure gold like unto pure glass. The foundations of the wall of the city were adorned with all manner of precious stones. And the twelve gates were twelve pearls; each of the several gates was of one pearl. And the street of the city was pure gold, as it were transparent glass.

"And I saw no temple therein, for the Lord God Almighty, and the Lamb, are the temple thereof. And the city had no need of the sun, neither of the moon to shine upon it; for the glory of God did lighten it, and the lamp thereof is the Lamb. And the nations shall walk amidst the light thereof.

"And there shall be no night there. And there shall in no wise enter into it anything unclean; but only they which are written in the Lamb's book of Life.

"And he showed me a river of water of life, bright as crystal, proceeding out of the throne of God and of the Lamb.

"In the midst of the street thereof, and on this side of the river and on that, was the tree of life, bearing twelve manner of fruits yielding its fruit every month: and the leaves of the tree were for the healing of the nations.

"And there shall be no curse any more; and the throne of God and of the Lamb shall be therein; and his servants shall serve Him. And they shall see His face, and His name shall be on their foreheads.

"And there shall be night no more; and they need no light of lamp, neither light of sun; for the Lord God shall give them light; and they shall reign forever and ever."

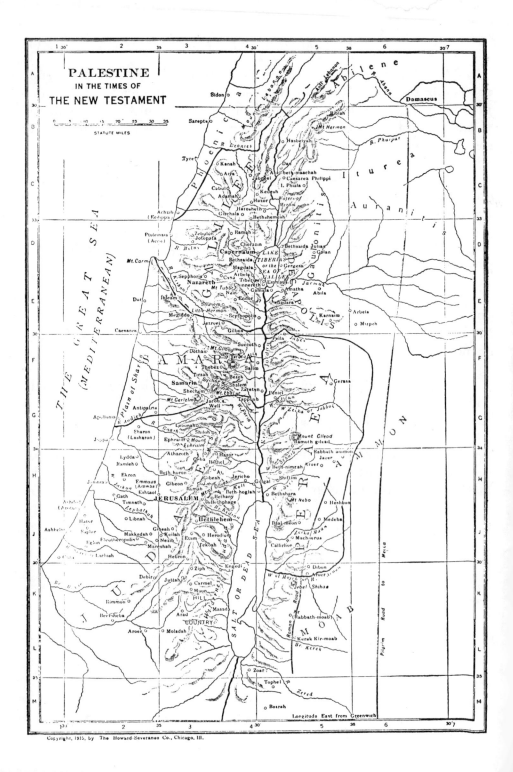

PALESTINE
IN THE TIMES OF
THE NEW TESTAMENT